The Hidden Prince

by

Billy Rennie

DORRANCE PUBLISHING CO., INC.
PITTSBURGH, PENNSYLVANIA 15222

The contents of this work including, but not limited to, the accuracy of events, people, and places depicted; opinions expressed; permission to use previously published materials included; and any advice given or actions advocated are solely the responsibility of the author, who assumes all liability for said work and indemnifies the publisher against any claims stemming from publication of the work.

All Rights Reserved
Copyright © 2011 by Fedderate R Investments Ltd.

No part of this book may be reproduced or transmitted, downloaded, distributed, reverse engineered, or stored in or introduced into any information storage and retrieval system, in any form or by any means, including photocopying and recording, whether electronic or mechanical, now known or hereinafter invented without permission in writing from the publisher.

Dorrance Publishing Co., Inc.
701 Smithfield Street
Pittsburgh, PA 15222
Visit our website at *www.dorrancebookstore.com*

ISBN: 978-1-4349-1208-4
eISBN: 978-1-4349-3917-3

Dedication

In memory of Sheena Rennie (Cowe) from the Blue Baby.
"Honesty is the sword toward being supreme."

Contents

	Page
Introduction	ix
Preface	xi
The Highland Home	1
The Beginning	3
Old Jock's Story	6
Queen Victoria	10
Hanton/Leys Marriage - Spinning the Web of Deception	12
Living Above Their Means - But Where Did the Money Come From?	15
The Marriage	19
Horses' Pedigree	23
John Hanton	25
Tracing John Hanton's Movements - Where He Lived from Birth to Death	28
Old Jock's Death	32
John Brown's Death	34
Jack Hanton - Uncle of My Wife, Sheena	36
Francis Hanton - Aunt of My Wife, Sheena	38
Sheena Mary Cowe	39
The John Brown Statue	42
The Stair Window of Crathie Manse	45

Hanton Profile - Family Members	47
Watch and Chain Masonic – Modern Day Technology	49
The Headstone	50
Pananich or Pannanich	52
Ballater	55
Our Family Bibles	57
John Brown's Parents	59
The Family Tree at a Glance	61
Proof – The Story So Far	64
The Throne	66
Queen Victoria's Grief Revealed in Letters	68
The Leys Family	71
Cousin John Brown	73
John Brown's CV at a Glance	75
Crathie Naird	79
Crathie Manse	81
John Brown – Intestate	84
John Brown's Birthplace – Crathie Naird	86
William McCombie – Cattle Breeder	89
Ballater Church	92
Crathie Church	94
Rabb – The Sheep Farmer – The Chance Meeting	95
The Thoughts of a Direct Descendent – Great, Great-Grandchild of the Prince	97
Norman MacLeod's Bust	99
Closed Doors and Questions	100

Introduction

The historical background and fascination within the Victorian era has lead to a wide variety of published information. Many have centred their research on Queen Victoria herself and the entourage of people surrounding her inspiring life.

The speculation and gossip mongering toward the possibility of marriage and siblings to the famous Scottish gillie John Brown has been hailed as a tale of secrecy and romance.

Evidence being destroyed or kept out of reach has not enabled the researchers, through time, to grasp firmly onto the truth and they find themselves left to envisage a picture of controversial matter, which would include guided and controlled information.

The story has never been completed in its entirety when viewing it from the outside in, but on this occasion the research and information supplied for your perusal has been supported from the inside out, which gives vital key information not readily attainable from elsewhere.

The tale of Mr. and Mrs. Brown began as a whisper in social circles of the time, then grew in substance with various mentions in press related articles, personal accounts, and diaries.

On reaching modern day, the romantic mystery surrounding the couple is still as prominent as ever and inspired a film release, which quite openly hinted of more between them.

Until this point, the avenue of research looked to be exhausted, but a member of the related family has now decided to unlock the secrets of the relationship and provide the concluding chapter to this fascinating part of our history.

Scotland is rich in historic and cultural background from the common man working the crofts, supplemented by fishing, beautiful scenery, Highlanders, the clearances, clans folk and their fighting abilities, battles, royalty, inventors, whiskey, engineering, music, romance, and passion, to mention a few. It is a proud nation welcomed globally and stands true to heart, proud and free.

Our clan chiefs were of high standing and the said John Brown was a man of high morals, honesty, and was admirable in his abilities of straight talking to any party that he felt might require it. This was unnerving to some, who felt it unfitting behavior by a servant, but in reality he was far more than this and, although the truth was kept secret, he stood tall to his challengers, having the difficult conversations with full support of Queen Victoria.

Any man of Scotland was and is born with the given right to protect his family, his home, his name, and himself. This he did and had to do on several occasions of his life, so we should all hold him in high regard.

A fitting couple who endured and protected their glimpse of normality in the hostility of the day, reigning triumphantly while able to have a private, secluded life in the heartlands of Scotland. And, what of the Prince? … Read on!

Preface

It was mentioned while compiling this publication that claiming an ancestor was a royal secret child was like shouting to the world that you have a unicorn at the bottom of your garden. The only problem is that the person, who claims author to this story from the past, is indeed most credible. An insight into his background is given prior to sifting through the memories and information provided, so you may judge the character and standing of this man for yourself.

- Brought up on the family farm with every day a working one, when not within school hours.
- Before and after leaving school, had won many major championships for show jumping in both juvenile and adult sections.
- Trained horses in the United States, Canada, Newfoundland, and in the UK, which included the winner of the first televised show jumping event at Wembley in the UK, and beating the likes of top show jumpers David Broom and Harvey Smith.
- Junior boxing champion for the Gordon Highlander Army Cadets.
- Married at twenty years of age to a staff registered nurse.
- Worked on pipelines driving bulldozers, diggers, trucks, and worked as a charge hand for some time with Dobson's of Edinburgh.
- Followed on to work in the ordinance survey as a civil servant for more than ten years, which took him behind the

closed doors of many exclusive, private estates in Scotland, including the highlands and islands. This also had him involved in the first usage of infrared photography within this sector.
- After redundancy came, he entered into management posts in Great Universal Stores and A & D Furnishings.
- Finished his working life as a driving assessor with a major Aberdeen service company prior to retiring due to ill health, being registered disabled and requiring increasing volumes of medication and hospital visitation (still ongoing).

In his spare time, there were many areas covered and accomplishments reached, which included the following:

- Chairman of the Local Community Council.
- Managed a Scottish show band with good success.
- Produced and presented a program on Scottish culture music on WAVES Radio for over eight years.
- Various publications in the local and nationally organized papers, which included special publications of historical topics, and was the supplier of information and involved in several books that successfully went to print.
- Was heavily involved in a BBC program called *Scotland's Greatest Mysteries*, which was a six-part series with two stories in each part that included the ancient arts and mysteries of the horseman's grip and word.
- Widely and highly regarded in the NE of Scotland as a local historian.
- Classed as one of Scotland's top commentators in specialized motor sports and truck festivals featuring wheelie trucks, jet trucks, car crushing, and tractor pulling, which took in work with television productions *U Bet* and *Record Breakers*.
- Worked with many well-known personalities like Roy Castle, Sheryl Baker, Richard Branson, Hughie Green, and Bernie Winters.
- Been in direct circles of interest formally and informally, which cover various members of UK and Scottish parliament, including leading members of the SNP; QCs—

Lairds, Ladies, Baron, Baroness—from various corners of the UK and Ireland; and entertainers, which included The Tartan Lads, Moira Kerr, Jonnie Beatty, Calum Kennedy, Robert Lovie, Robbie Sheppard, and Gordon Pattillo, not to mention Slim Whitman and George Hamilton IV.
- ➤ Charity fund-raising over the years to what would have been quite an amount of assistance to the deserving causes.
- ➤ Chief of the Clan Rennie, Sept of the Clan "MacDonnell of Keppoch"—a proud and distinguished Scotsman.

Some accomplishments you may agree, which only a few might achieve and, for sure, an educated life of great variance.

Within the last few members of the society of "horseman" known only by grip and word, and being, at times, a travelling man, he is found to be a "Fellow Brother we may trust."

The Highland Home

Balmoral Castle on the Balmoral Estate in Aberdeenshire

This is still the Royal Family's holiday home today and is open to the public from April to July every year. It is well worth visiting with the ballroom holding many artefacts of interest, including some of John Browns. Queen Victoria loved this residence and the people surrounding it.

To this day, it is openly stated that the Royal Family is very proud of their Scottish heritage, the "fine folk" of the surrounding areas. Their own large stretch of the river with good fishing is but a stone's throw away from the residency.

The shooting rights and handsome acreage are more predominantly used for deer and pheasant (game hunting). Spectacular views take in all the natural beauty and riches of Royal Deeside. There are stable facilities for the horses and carriages and grounds with secluded areas in which to walk even on a busy tourist open day. A large selection of wild life abounds, including birds of prey and foliage of such variance and beauty.

When visiting, you can feel why there is and was a fondness for this Highland Home. It is no wonder that this prime, but secluded area became like a fairy tale castle after reconstruction and design changes by Albert and Victoria.

In winter, it sure is like a wonderland of unspoiled, breathtaking views—as it is in all seasons, a treasure in the eye of the beholder.

The Beginning

Upon taking a trip to Aberdeen Royal Infirmary from Lonmay to visit my sick mother back in 1968, it wasn't such a big deal, but I wasn't prepared for the heartfelt, historical trip I was going to experience in future years; a trip that would take me back in time and then stay with me until my dying day.

My mother was cared for by a nurse named Sheena who was in her late teens and hailed from Strathdon. As fate would have it, she was to become my wife and two years later she bore me two fine sons.

While we were still settling into marriage when the boys were young, we did several sorties up Donside and into Deeside. It was the first of these trips that Sheena wanted to visit her grandparents where they lived in a small flat in Tarland.

Visiting them was like stepping back in time; everything in the house was as old as the folks themselves, and their mannerisms were the same. Sheena had me well warned about the "Dos and Don'ts", and after the introduction was over, the ladies went to the good room and Jock and I went into the kitchen.

This practice was the "norm" in the northeast of Scotland, and now today it has all gone by the wayside … perhaps for the good.

Sheena's grandparents' surname was Hanton, and I was asked by my host to call him Jock. Myself being from an agricultural background, having spent time in the army cadets, and also having boxed and shot for the Gordon Highlanders (Bridge of Don Barracks and Barry Budden and Redford Barracks at

Edinburgh), I had it cracked. The old man opened up to me with some of his old tales, and wondrous tales they were. We talked more than my own grandfather had talked to me.

"Old Jock," as he was fondly called by his family, had a stoop, but in his younger day stood over six feet tall and was well built. He was a glutton for any challenge, large or small. He had service with the Gordon's during World War I, and because of his stature he openly admitted he got away with lying about his age to join up.

On a charge, he got a bullet through one forearm, shattering a bone that was later removed, leading to his discharge from service.

Jock had a smallholding on Deeside (a croft), but was unable to do much manual work with his disability. Jock lived a quiet life, relying on his loving wife to look after him. She bore him four children--Jack, Molly, Francis and Margaret.

Molly and Francis took after their father, moody and sharp with their tongues, and kept a grudge for a long time. The other two, Jack and Margaret, were outgoing, friendly, and also very helpful, but they also had a mischievous sense of humor. No one was aware that Margaret was slightly deformed and had to wear a specially made corset to hide this deformity.

They were all brought up with their heads held high with strict morals that included the utmost in courtesy and common decency, which was admirable and proved to be very well respected by friends and colleagues alike.

Old Jock could not get out of Tarland a lot, and for whatever reason, his immediate family did not spend a lot of time with him. Sheena and I having a car had a lot of fun taking him and Granny around their old haunts, visiting houses, farms, hotels, and people. Then one day, out of the blue, came a story that had us sworn to secrecy, but forty-four years later, I believe I am released from that promise.

Old Jock and his brother have passed away and are long gone. In Jock's immediate family, two have passed away and the two remaining are no longer interested in what happens. Some of his grandchildren are no longer with us, and it was only when his great-grandchildren asked questions not so long ago, it was realized they would like the truth about their family background.

While visiting a small graveyard on Deeside, Jock could hardly speak, and there were tears in his eyes. Giving him his own time he opened up and told me he was in his family's graveyard.

A six-foot high wall surrounded the graves, and one-by-one he told me who was who and their relationships. Lay resting were Hantons, Leys, and Browns, etc.... None of the names made sense to me, until Jock started to tell me the story of Queen Victoria and John Brown. Brown was born on a farm near Crathie in 1826 on December 8 (Crathie Naird), second of eleven children to farmer John Brown (1790-1875) and wife, Margaret Leys (1799-1876).

Young John Brown found employment as a farmworker/estate worker on Sir Robert Gordon's estate at Balmoral, and was retained by the Royals when they acquired the Balmoral Estate. John Brown then worked first as a gillie and then leader of Queen Victoria's pony.

Old Jock explained that the relationship between John Brown and Queen Victoria was the subject of speculation and gossip between the politicians of the day, especially with the Queen's absence from royal duties and her preference to stay at Balmoral.

Among the locals at Ballater, the Queen was often referred to as Mrs. Brown as locals were familiar in seeing them together; all gossip faded as they were accepted as a couple and could continue their business with little or no fuss.

As we moved from grave to grave, Old Jock, fighting back tears and talking with a dry throat, explained who was who. With me just listening and taking it all in, I couldn't help but wonder what this man was made of and the life he had to lead—knowing the truth about himself and where he came from, but sworn to secrecy by those with power. Here I was with an old man pouring his heart out. Old Jock, his sister Mary, his brother Alexander, and his parents John and Mary, did not exist in reality, but they did and were raised in secret in an area named Pannanich.

Old Jock's Story

Jock's story goes like this ... John Brown and Queen Victoria did have a baby boy, raised by a housemaid by the name of Leys-Hanton. The Hantons were given an allowance every year to look after the boy and his education, but they were sworn to secrecy the same as we were. They were given a "great big house with lots of windows and a lot of good quality furniture and bedding."

The boy's first name was John after his father (John Brown), but had adopted the surname of Hanton.

Old Jock had a smile on his face and a half-hearted laugh when he told me the Queen always dressed in loose-fitted clothes and was said to be overweight; little did they suspect that she was heavy with child (Jock's father) and that was the reason she spent a lot of time at Balmoral.

Jock was full of mixed feelings every time I spoke to him, although he was hurt about his background he took great pride in it as well, and often loved to dwell on the subject with me.

John Brown was ill with Erysipelas, which covered most of his face and had a high fever. Sadly, he passed away on March 29—Tuesday at 10:40 P.M. in 1883. As old Jock said, sadly these were the times he lived in and what everyone had to endure, such was the loyalty to the Royals as the child and his family were only spoken about behind closed doors.

History tells us that there is no evidence of John Brown and Queen Victoria having a sexual relationship, but as I had first-hand insight with the Hanton family and indeed many years in the company of Jock Hanton, I find no reason to doubt the old man's story, especially when he called John Brown his grandfather and Queen Victoria his grandmother.

Armed with these historical facts, some researchers and I set out to try and trace some documents and unearth some further truth about the story before it became myth and possibly lost forever. We have no intention in bringing any disrespect to any person or persons, but it would be nice to get the family recognized. It would be no disgrace to open up to the parentage, or accept the facts as they stand. We do not display a frown over such matters in common day society and to be honest, a little excitement and romance is such a well-understood area we can all relate to.

I am not a descendant of the family, but I am greatly interested in historical on-goings and so-called "mysteries." Although this is no mystery, I would like to clear up one or two points of fact and let you into the secrets of the past.

Old Jock standing tall in the doorway of Carriers Croft with his father, Prince John, to the right.

ALFORD COUPLE'S GOLDEN WEDDING

Mr and Mrs John Hanton, Wright's Croft, Breda, Alford, received from their family a pair of easy chairs as a golden wedding gift.

A native of Pannanich, Ballater, Mr Hanton was road foreman at Strathdon for 34 years, retiring about 12 years ago. Since then he has had Wright's Croft. Mrs Hanton belongs to Strathdon.

Though now both over 70 years of age, Mr and Mrs Hanton still cycle regularly into Alford for their shopping. They have a family of two sons and four daughters, one of the sons being Mr A. B. Hanton, 27 Castle Street, Forres, who has a grocery business. Three grandsons are in the Gordon Highlanders.

Prince John and his beloved wife reach their Golden Wedding Anniversary.
(Within another newspaper article, it was reported and verified they received a purse containing gold sovereigns as a gift. From whom?)

Old Jock as a young man in the Gordon Highlanders.

Carriers Croft where Jock Hanton lived, which is less than fifty meters from Wrights Croft in Alford.)

Wrights Croft where Prince John lived, as it looks today.

Queen Victoria

Victoria was born in Kensington Palace in London on May 24, 1819, and took the throne in 1837. Barely eighteen years old, she showed a wilful stubbornness and on February 10, 1840, she married her cousin Prince Albert.

We can only surmise that they had a fantastic sexual life as she bore him nine children, but Queen Victoria became increasingly more difficult to live with, prone to self-pity and strong prejudices.

We can only surmise that in the Queen's early thirties, she like other young women, was still healthy and with respect had an eye for a good-looking young male. With John Brown being seven years younger, attentiveness and flirtation took over, with Albert often out stalking, shooting, and partaking in his many other interests. It would be no surprise when their relationship blossomed.

Let us at this stage be realistic; after nine children and sleeping with the same partner, familiarity must have set in even though the Queen loved Albert very much. The sense of adventure, mystery, and excitement in a life of solitude rendered her susceptible or perhaps at the time, she had the longing to find out what it is like to make love to another man. After all, she had only known the soft touches of one man (Albert). Was the queen enjoying a second womanhood? Perhaps John Brown's attentiveness was seen as a flirtation, something Prince Albert didn't do. Did his toddy of whiskey and water help to throw caution to the wind, or was it the fact that Prince Albert was often made wretched by his loneliness in exile, going off on his own to find solitude, which was sometimes for days on end.

Out of all the people we have talked to and the stories that have been heard, it was reflected that Prince Albert decided to keep Queen Victoria pregnant. He was often unavailable for things he didn't want to do, and was known for his lame excuses, e.g., migraines and rheumatism and in the long run was described as a hypochondriac.

Prince Albert was known to shake the bed with other women and his royal friends chose him a favorite. A woman named Catherine Walters or "Skittles," as she was known. The Marquis of Harrington kept her for many years, the eldest son of the seventh Duke of Devonshire (Spencer Compton Cavendish).

It is not known or recorded within the close royal circles, but there is great belief that Victoria and Albert during the mid-1850s were drifting apart, Albert getting bored with humdrum and trivial matters, and the Queen getting and enjoying attention from a young fit man (John Brown). By this time John Brown was in attendance at picnics, and expeditions, to places such as Invermark, Fettercairn, Glen Fishy, Dalwhinnie, and Blair Atholl. Was there a last attempt by Victoria and Albert to patch things up on these visits or was there something more critical going on out in the public eye while keeping up appearances?

The reason this question must be asked is due to the records traced on Old Jock Hanton's father, one of which as written states, "John Hanton, born 6th Nov 1861 at Loinahaun Glengairn to George Hanton and Mary Leys - domestic servant." The boy was born four weeks before Prince Albert died.

Hanton/Leys Marriage
Spinning the Web of Deception

To set a trap for a mouse, most people put in a piece of cheese, which will not remain attractive, but if you use a piece of chocolate as bait it will retain its color and flavoring; it's the same with doing research about the Hanton family story. As one tale may go stale and cold, we could eventually find another tasty morsel to enlighten our pallet. That is what we found when we started out on our research into George Hanton and Mary Leys.

Their wedding took place on February 16, 1861, at Loinahaun Glengairn in the Church of Scotland. George Hanton, at the time, was a farmworker aged twenty-four years and Mary Leys (aunt of John Brown) worked as a domestic servant aged twenty-seven years. George's father George was deceased, but Elizabeth Symon, his mother, was still alive; Mary's father, John, was a weaver and her mother was also called Mary.

The minister who performed the ceremony was called Robert Neil (Missionary Minister on Royal Bounty, Glengairn) and the two witnesses were related to the couple on the bride's side; they were John Coutts and Hugh Brown. What a cozy little nest and a wedding approximately eight months before the child John was born.

It was revealed to us that Mary Leys (wife of George Hanton) was especially chosen to raise the boy and give him a good education in English and other worldly subjects. Perhaps, this is another of Scotland's best-kept secrets, but with so many cryptic clues, it was only a matter of time before they were deciphered.

Mary Leys-Hanton was well spoken and educated in the finer things in life such as reading, manners, languages, religion, etiquette, eating, and dress. All these things were then passed onto Prince John and the rest of the family.

The 1851 Census shows us that Mary Leys was seventeen years old and described as a student scholar, which confirms the stories that were told about the boy John having a good education with a good grounding in his early years for his long and hectic life, which saw him working on his croft at Alford in Aberdeenshire until his death at Wrights Croft, Alford, on [h] December 27, 1942, aged eighty-one years.

Prince John was well taught about who his real parents were and at an early age, was told to keep it a secret, but how could he when Queen Victoria and John Brown made frequent visits to him at Pannanich and enquired after the family and their welfare. Visits were also made by the resident minister, to which the boy would reportedly hide under the table and not come out until he was gone.

This is possibly the most referenced and familiar picture of the couple together. Although she loved Albert dearly, the flame between them must have dwindled and only been kept alive by correctness in the public eye. The "Queen's Highland Servant" rose to be the most influential member of the royal household, which is no real surprise with him being the "man oh the hoose."

Living Above Their Means
But Where Did the Money Come From?

Going forward in time to find out more about John Hanton, the Census for 1881 was consulted for the areas of Glenmuick and Pannanich Cottages. By this time, all the Hanton family are recorded, but John Hanton has disappeared from the age of twenty ... where is he?

George Hanton (farm servant) and Mary Leys (domestic servant) were married at the Loinahaun Glengairn Church of Scotland in 1861.

There is another question to be asked. How on earth did George Hanton earn a possible three shillings a year as a farm laborer, manage to raise a family and feed, cloth, and educate them? Where did all the money come from?

There were so many stories requiring clarity, and the findings when visiting Balmoral, Crathie, Ballater, and Braemar, gave the feeling that everything is talked about in whispers. The generations of locals all know the stories, but prefer to let sleeping dogs lie, but it was found that if you ask the right questions at the right time, you will get the truth, or near to it.

John Brown's mother was Leys, and the baby was placed in the care of George Hanton and his wife Mary Leys. Mary and her sister Margaret were both domestic servants and records place them to be John Brown's aunts. When Margaret died her will read:

To my sister Mary Leys-Hanton, wife of George Hanton, residing at Broom Cottage, Pannanich Village, Ballater, I bequeath…

		£	S	D
Cash in house	-	3	1	8
	-	8	15	3
Total	-	11	16	11

<u>Abroad</u>

Eleven shares of the capitalized instalment stock of the Freehold Loan and Savings Company of Toronto

<u>Value</u>   -   £11

Three shares of the capitalized stock of same company.

<u>Value</u>   -   £60

Grand Total= £105-6-11

Margaret passed away on June 22, 1897; this according to records, would only have made her forty-six years old and interesting to note, she never married. She would only have been twenty years of age when the child was born.

It is interesting to find out what a domestic servant's wages would have been for that time, and it turns out to be somewhere between two to four shillings per year, enough to just live and get buy each day without having the luxury of being able to save. Taking the bull by the horns, I made some enquiries into monetary value, investments, and banking of the day. Back in those days, domestic staff would seldom be entertained by banking facilities as they had very little or no money, and only the higher-class gentry would have access to information on investments. It was then asked what the present day's value of £105-6-11p would be, and was told at a guess that today's value would be fifty-five thousand pounds, approximated using the GDP per capita conversion system of monetary value.

Where would a domestic servant gain the information on investments in banking, especially abroad? A bank advisor made it known that this type of knowledge and ability would have to come from some influential person with money and contacts.

"Where would a domestic servant get such a large sum to invest?" was asked in return. Perhaps a child was involved; it could have been payoff money or a retainer with an allowance every quarter year. We were shocked. Was Margaret, who was seven years younger than her sister Mary, the go-between to look after the baby's interests? On her death, did the young man have to fend for himself as he was taught throughout his upbringing?

Our research shows that George and Mary Leys were still living at Broom Cottage in 1901 (ages sixty-four and sixty-six), and an interesting fact is that they employed a domestic servant by the name of Mary Coutts.

In May of 1915, the supposed parents of John Hanton were living apart—George still at Broom Cottage Pannanich and Mary at 15 Forbes St. Aberdeen.

George Hanton, Born 1837 - Died February 28, 1920 (age eighty-three).
Mary Leys, Born 1834 - Died May 10, 1916 (aged eighty-two).

It is widely believed that Margaret Leys, housemaid to Queen Victoria, presented a baby boy to her sister Mary and he was brought up as Mary and George Hanton's firstborn, but in reality the firstborn was, in fact, George Hanton born three years later in 1864 and died March 26, 1949, at age eighty-five at Burn O'Vat. This makes sense as firstborn males in those days were named after their father.

The story unravels itself. Queen Victoria to John Brown (1861), the housemaid Margaret Leys and her sister Mary Leys-Hanton were in on the secret and agreed to raise the child as a Hanton, and although all the locals around Crathie and Ballater knew of the child, until today it has been the best kept secret in Scotland.

Mary and Margaret Leys were indeed John Brown's aunts, with Margaret's accumulated fortune coming from the royal purse and John Brown's. This money was for looking after the child and his education, "hush" money, as some people would call it.

Another thought is that the boss of the glen was Queen Victoria's confidante, and John Brown's mother, whose maiden name was Leys. Was she the brains behind the prince's disappearance in November 1861?

A hidden cottage above Pannanich Wells, in the forest at the other side of the hill lays a secret that was the first house in which the Hantons lived. It was out of sight, but not out of mind, yet it was still reachable by pony cart.

The Marriage

Over the years, much speculation about John Brown and Queen Victoria streamed through Europe, as well as Britain. Those close to the couple talked about Mr. and Mrs. Brown. Victoria's family joked about Mama's lover and her daughters made great fun of the situation.

Letters that the Queen wrote and entries into her journals showed a strong sense of feeling between the couple. If you look at the similarities between Victoria's treatment of Albert and Brown in death, they are too numerous to ignore.

Many references have been made to the couple having married. The strongest was when they had a long holiday in Luzern in Switzerland in August 1868 where they checked in under a pseudonym.

Armed with some snippets of information of a wedding and surrounding gossip being picked up, we tried to get names of people who would have accompanied the Queen and John Brown. One such person who stands out was duchess and wife of the sixth Duke of Athol, who was a member of court and mistress of the robes; the story goes that she witnessed the wedding.

We thought we were drawing a blank in getting evidence to the theory of a wedding, when we stumbled on the name Reverend Norman MacLeod, D.D., a Royal Chaplain of Scotland in 1857 and a trusted friend of Queen Victoria. You can see him greeting Queen Victoria with relief on her statue in George Square on the occasion of her visit to the cathedral in Edinburgh.

Reverend Norman MacLeod was born in 1812 and died in 1872 and, during that time, was chaplain to Queen Victoria from 1857 to 1872. He was moderator of the general assembly of the Church of Scotland, Doctor of Divinity, and Dean of the Order of the Thistle. In all, he was a very educated man with strong convictions and a belief in his work and widely respected by all who met him.

It is our belief that a marriage did take place and whether it was Luzern in Switzerland or in Scotland, it doesn't really matter. Let us explain further if we can. John Brown and Queen Victoria definitely stayed in Luzern in Switzerland and included in the party where Reverend Norman MacLeod, three of Victoria's children (Louise, Beatrice, and Leopold), as well as secretaries, cooks, maids, etc. … in August 1868 that size of a party couldn't be hidden, even if the Queen used a pseudonym.

This story has two twists, the first being that Reverend Norman MacLeod made a deathbed confession repenting his action in presiding over Queen Victoria's marriage to John Brown.

An article that appeared in the *Daily Mail* September 2, 2006, relates that Woodrow Wyatt met Queen Elizabeth the Queen Mother in the 1980s. On one occasion she claimed she found documents in the royal archives at Windsor suggesting that Victoria and John Brown did indeed get married.

Both stories we believe to be true and once again during the research it came upon us to be entrusted with a secret, the person and the place we promised never to reveal, but we believe we know where the bans for the royal wedding lie. This cryptic clue is here to view:

"The royal connections are no doubt
Clever at what they are about,
But everything in its simplicity
Can be seen in all its dignity.
The Rev. MacLeod to his grave did go,
And so a story of long ago.
The marriage bans, what a hoot!
They are cleverly hidden up his spoot.
You will not see them for dust,
If you find MacLeod or bust."

A young descendant from the Hanton family and I held them in our hands, but only time will reveal them unless you can override a royal order.

My researcher and I are aware of where the marriage ceremony took place; we have visited the location, been shown round the room and also a small room where a small reception was held, but we were sworn to secrecy and must for the time being stick to our words and actions. This we did before God.

Queen Victoria's orders were that the marriage bans must not be removed from the building and their hiding place be kept secret. For those who want to pursue this piece of history, we can tell you that the wedding took place on a Sunday. For many it was no secret, but you like me will find that to start research on this subject is very difficult; you have to unravel all the riddles to let the picture slowly emerge.

The two rooms that the wedding and the reception took place in, were especially commissioned as an extension to the existing building, with a commanding view over the grounds and the River Dee (some few miles from Balmoral). We have revealed all that is allowed without breaking our word to God, but if history fascinates you, then please read on, as every word is factual. None of it is made up or fictional and the clues are there for you to find. If you are like us, then take a little time and do some research, but be advised to tread softly and try not to upset too many people, as they still want to keep the closet closed and the skeletons at peace within it.

"Mi\le fa\ilte dhuit le d'bhre/id,
Fad do re/ gun robh thu sla\n.
Mo/ran la\ithean dhuit is si\th,
Le d'mhaitheas is le d'ni\ bhi fa\s."

Translation

"A thousand welcomes to you with your marriage
kerchief, may you be healthy all your days.
May you be blessed with long life and peace,
may you grow old with goodness, and with riches."

ReverendNorman MacLeod

There are diaries containing a report that one of the Queen's chaplains, Norman MacLeod, D.D. (The Highlanders' Friend), made a deathbed confession repenting for his action in presiding over Queen Victoria's marriage to John Brown. This is recorded in the recently discovered diaries of Lewis Harcourt, a politician of the time.

He also published a children's book, *The Golden Thread* in 1861, which makes interesting reading (notice the year and story line). This would seem to have been released to mark the year and tell the story of a lost prince in the woods that had to get past many obstacles and tests in life before being able to return home.

"It was this, they trusted God and did what was right," but holding fast on the golden thread led them in a way of peace and safety.

Unfortunately, in real life this was not to be for the prince in question, however. God was trusted wholeheartedly and the parents were only answerable to God!

Horses' Pedigree

Leaving no stone unturned and trying to delve into every angle in our quest for answers to enlighten the descendants of John Hanton, we turned to the conclusion that Victoria and her family wanted us servants to eventually find the truth.

Tracing a royal pedigree of horses from 1863 we got the shock of our lives, upon asking the question, Who is behind this lot? What is happening, as it can't just be a coincidence? Is someone having a joke or are they spelling it out in front of us? On showing the pedigree to some of the Hanton family, they couldn't believe their eyes. Take a look at some of the pedigree horses and some of their names:

Hanton	Old Jock
Windsor	Raise a Secret
Bloomer	Jocky Hafling
Grey Breasted Jock	Monarch
Queen Mother	Oh La Ray

These are just the basic names that were of interest to the research required, but all the rest are related to the Queen Victoria story. Work it out for yourselves and form your own opinion.

Old Jock	John Brown's Father
Windsor	The Castle Name
Captain	Lord Dalkeith
Panmure	Secretary of State for War

Bloomer	It definitely was, don't you think?
Hanton	Pat/Lizzie
Raise a Secret	Self-explanatory, don't you think?
Oh La Ray	Translation says it all?
Queen Mother	Self-explanatory
Grey Breasted Jock	John Brown
Jocky Hafling	The Young Prince – John Brown (Hanton)?
Rob Roy McGregor	Paddle Streamer Used by the Queen

John Hanton

Son of Queen Victoria and John Brown, as many records show, he was born on the November 6, 1861, supposedly at Loinahaun, Glengairn.

Supposed or adopted parents were George Hanton (farm servant) and Mary Leys-Hanton, but from John Hanton's birth to the 1881 Census, the Hanton family was living in Broom Cottage, Pannanich. Having visited the properties and trying to understand the family move from farming to crofter/contractor and working from Broom Cottage, creates thoughts in our minds about John Hanton's supposed parents.

How did they raise seven children and run a business, as well as move into a substantial building like Broom Cottage built of dress stone, as opposed to an old clay biggin on a farm.

Whatever lay behind the scenes, Pannanich would have been a good place to raise someone of royal blood, as Ballater was not yet developed and to get across the river, you had to wade or use the ferry. I suppose if you had not been for the development of the "spa" at Pannanich and the requirement for accommodations, there would have been no Ballater of today. It is known that the boy prince was well catered to as a youth, living in a healthy environment with "spa" waters and simple food.

John Hanton married Mary Ann Anderson on January 23, 1892, at Parkstile, Strathdon. They had seven in the family:

> John Hanton Jr. (1893-1977),
> Mary Ann Hanton (1895-1934),
> and Alexander B. Hanton (1901-1992)

Although the three above are shown on the 1901 Census, these others are not:

> George Hanton (1892-1892) lived seven days,
> Helen Anderson Hanton (1895-1954),
> Eliza Jane Hanton (1904-1990),
> and Isabella Hanton (1907-1992).

In the 1901 Census for Strathdon - Claverhouse, John Hanton is seen to be employed as a road foreman at twenty-nine years of age, and many stories have emerged about him and his escapades. For instance, he always carried a garden rake on his bicycle; it took years for people to find out that he used it for poaching salmon on his way to and from work. John Hanton's father often talked about his big house and his little house, his big house being Broom Cottage, Pannanich, Ballater, and his small house being at Newton Cottage, Crathie, and Braemar.

Newton Cottage was a small dwelling with an earth floor, open fire, and thatched roof; usually everyone slept in one room.

Broom Cottage was totally up-market, built from dressed stone and lime with several windows and rooms. Research tells us that Newton Cottage was owned, but Broom Cottage was a tenancy for George's lifetime only, a tenancy he held until his death in 1920. This was a tenancy from a royal hand for the upbringing of John Hanton, the prince.

Keeping in mind that George Hanton was a farm worker, he also managed to leave upon his death the total of £124, and this sum was shared equally among his offspring. Twenty thousand pounds approximated using the GDP per capita conversion system of monetary value, which is not a bad sum of money considering the job at hand was done and his comfortable livelihood had been sustained for years.

Once again, it comes up like a monster; a child, John Hanton brought up with George and Mary Leys and living in Newton Cottage? This was not correct or fitting for the secret child so they, the Hantons, moved into a dressed stone cottage then called Broom Cottage, Pannanich, with an upstairs, fancy furniture, and lots of windows, which is still a nice building and stands in place today.

Broom Cottage, Pannanich, Ballater

Tracing John Hanton's Movements
Where He Lived from Birth to Death

John Brown's mother stayed at the settlement of Crathienaird, which can be found using the following:

> Continue on the B976 from Crathie to Gairnshiel Lodge, travelling north. In a few miles, you will come to where the river Gairn comes down from the hills and runs along the left-hand side of the road as you are travelling. Prior to this point there is a track to your left, which takes you into uninhabited areas and long abandoned settlements. This was once a fairly large area of settled land with several small villages within the communities. Going up this left hand track off the main road off B976 for at least a mile, you will be in the area known as Loinahaun.

The remains of the township of Loinahaun, Glengairn are situated on the northeast facing terrace by the right bank of River Gairn as depicted in the first edition area ordinance survey map of 1869). This inhabitancy was comprised of eleven buildings, of which three were unroofed, and at least three garden enclosures, but sadly were reduced to footings and recorded as such from the 1970s ordinances survey maps, but aerial photography clearly defines the township and crofts positions of layout across the given ground.

  The area is mainly used for grouse shooting now, but this is where the newly born prince spent his first eighteen to twenty-four months. Hidden in the forest, halfway down a mountain, but in easy reach of his grandmother (John Brown's mother and sister of Mary Hanton - Margaret Leys), being but a mere brisk walk south on the same road at Crathienaird, with the watchful eye and security of Balmoral Castle and estates only a stone's throw away, just like the family story portrays.

This area is interestingly right next to the edge of Cairngorms National Park and confirmed by the first place the child was registered, quiet, secluded, and seemingly free from prying eyes or gossip.

After the initial times of circumstance containment passed and the "lovers cover up" was concealed by the loyal and faithful, the allotted parents, namely George and Mary Hanton, moved down the hill from Loinahaun, Glengairn to Newton Cottage being his "small house" and in the same area of time had Broom Cottage in Pannanich (his big house where John Hanton spent approximately twenty-seven years). It also was where Margaret Leys, John's granny lived until she died. It must at this point be said that for a working/servant class family to have this type of accommodations at that time, throws a big question mark again on where the money came from.

After John Hanton got married, he moved to a small house at Milton of Forberg, Glengairn. This was indeed closer to the Estate of Balmoral and their place of residence for approximately three years from 1893 to 1896. In this abode, their first child was born—John Hanton Jr., "Auld Jock."

At this point, it must be said that his real father, John Brown, had died in 1883 and his mother was in the latter years of her life (respectfully deceased in 1901). It could be surmised that there was minimal interest shown to John, who found himself losing any chance of recognition and the passionately entangled knowledge of who he was, starting to drive him a bit further away from home (maybe sick at the site of what should have been his birthright).

Claver House croft on Donside was their new home:

> Take the A97 from Dinnet and head north passing Boultenstone Hotel on your right. At the top of the hill, you will come to a crossroads. Do a left, which has sign

posted HEUGH HEAD and drive a short distance 'til you see dotted crofts and houses.

It is here that some Hanton offspring down to some grandchildren were born who have been previously mentioned.

John Hanton and Mary Ann's next move was when John tired of working on the roads and took up residence down the hill, in the village of Bellabegg in Strathdon (found on the A994). This place was called Station Cottage, which still remains a dwelling house today.

This was, however, only for a short time until the "caretaker for the Lonach Hall" position was secured, which included the flat accommodation attached. It must be pointed out that their respect and services were so good that on retirement, he and his wife, Mary, were presented with a clock to mark their devoted service to the community. This clock is still held by the family today with pride of place.

Presented to Mr. and Mrs. Hanton by the Lonach Committee in recognition of services rendered as caretakers in April 1931.

This was indeed the final move for John Hanton, who then moved with his wife to Carrier's Croft beside his son "Auld Jock" in Wright's Croft just west of Alford until they passed away. The son and his wife then moved to a flat in Tarland and filled in the details to the reasons *The Beginning* occurred.

Records indicate the man's entire life, work, family, secret, and departure circled around two hills, namely Monagowan and Morven. In speaking to the older members of these community areas that knew John Hanton, they reserved their "passed" secret knowledge even to family members to only state, "I mine there was something aboot him, aye, definitely something."

John Hanton (the Prince) and his loving wife, Mary Ann, standing beside their car in all their finery at Lonach Hall where he remained as caretaker in his later years of life.

The car is a Landaulette in terms of body type, but there is not enough else shown for us to make a confirmed I.D. Even the door handle is not distinctive. This type of body was reserved for expensive cars. The rear portion folded away… like a pram hood. Daimler, Rolls, Albion, and Maudslay were popular locally among the aristocracy. Maudslay in particular, as Sir Charles Forbes of New, Strathdon, was their chairman. He influenced many of the local top set to buy Maudslays!

You can see, there is a reflection of a certain gentry in the car window. I wonder who it is?

Maybe a vintage car enthusiast could enlighten us as to the exact model of car, but for us the importance is showing, as throughout this book, the access to the fineries of what money can bring while the means was not achievable by common folk, unless they happened to be "catered for" to a point.

Old Jock's Death

In later years, Old Jock's (the prince's son) condition grew worse and his daughter Molly took him in at West Lodge on Dunecht Estate. He spent hours in the front room, grounded in his wheelchair, cutting and sticking things into a scrapbook. This was indeed a scrapbook that holds postcards of all the castles in Scotland. Obviously, all that he could lay his hands on, anyway. Wheeled in front of a green felted folding table, his feeble hands would set to work cutting out the little corners on each page of the book that would allow the insertion of each postcard, as they became available.

This was his way of holding Scotland in his hands, as his birthright would never let happen, but indeed a bittersweet reminder of where he came from. Some days done with cheer and joy and on other days done with a sour frown about his face, the torment of such knowledge taking its toll for sure.

Molly used to get playfully annoyed at his mess, however, as the little bits of paper went everywhere and she had no problem in letting him know that fact.

He soon passed away and members of the family got together to discuss and decide how the funeral arrangements were to be made and executed. They all gathered in the very same front room and not moments into the discussions, an almighty row broke out that would last for most of the afternoon.

The contents that sparked the fury was the fact that the "secret" of the family was brought up and how best they could word the grave to reflect the true standing of the man and his birthright without making it known to be an obvious statement. Well, Molly ended the dispute quite swiftly by making it quite plain to all. The words are still as fresh today as they were then and this is what she stated, "I am sick to death with this going on and on. Nothing's going to change how things are and if we bury him beside his father and put an inscription to suit, then that brings it alive all over again. This needs to be forgotten for our own good and end this bloody family tree and grave trails. He is getting cremated and that's that! It stops right now!"

Old Jock was cremated in Aberdeen on her solemn word and it was thought that the trails were then dislodged enough to dissolve the memory in due time.

From that day onward, it was never spoken about again … 'til now.

Old Jock's scrapbooks of his Scottish Kingdom still exist within the family to this day in original and mint condition.

John Brown's Death

He was a legendary drinker of bootleg whiskey in the Glen and any other whiskey on which he could lay his hands. Whiskey was used as a relaxant, but take too much and it was and still is like a drug with different effects on different people. In John, he could be pleasant and mannerly, but on the other hand, he could be damn rude.

The appointment of Sir James Reid as Queen Victoria's physician had an undermining affect on John Brown, as he no longer had full control. Sir James Reid was born in 1849 in the Aberdeenshire village called Ellon. He had distinguished learning at Aberdeen grammar school and university, practicing medicine in London and Vienna, with the additional benefit that German was a language he spoke fluently.

The Queen being insistent that her medical attendant must be a Scotsman, Sir James Reid was highly qualified, being able to converse with foreign heads of state and often dining in private with the Queen. Sadly John Brown and Sir James Reid did not get along.

On the morning of March 25, 1883, some eighteen months after Sir James Reid arrived at court, John Brown awoke with Erysipelas of the face coupled with delirium tremens. When John Brown passed away on March 27, Sir James Reid's name was on the death certificate.

Delirium tremens, otherwise known as DTS—alcohol withdrawal. The DTS can occur when a person does not eat enough food, but has had a period of heavy drinking. This can also occur when a person has had a history of heavy drinking and can be triggered by an infection, head injury, etc.

Treatment in most cases can be done by penicillin or antibiotics and, thus, eliminates the infection, but again a question arises. With Sir James Reid being an attendant at Windsor, why wasn't John Brown treated? Or, was it a pure political pact to get rid of him through his own doing? I suggest that a doctor of Sir James Reid's standing and education gave him the power to save John Brown, but he didn't.

Such was the standing of Sir James Reid's power in the royal court, which some twenty or more years later saw him given the task of retrieving letters of a confidential nature from George Profeit. The letters were to George's father from Queen Victoria regarding John Brown and apparently George was blackmailing King Edward VII.

It is said that some three hundred letters were in the box, but the King received only one hundred and fifty. The price paid for them was not disclosed. One of the more interesting letters from Sir James Reid disclosed that he had looked at some of the letters and "found them most compromising."

Was John Brown the Queen's stallion in her time of need when neglected by Prince Albert? Her lover, husband, protector, and confider, but at the same time, hated by the heads of state for his influence over the Queen. We all know that they were married and John was totally devoted to his wife, Queen Victoria, and that their child was placed in good and safe hands. The question is asked … At what price does royal love and devotion come with?

Jack Hanton
Uncle of My Wife, Sheena

William John Hanton, born on the January 4, 1922, was the son of Old Jock Hanton, born October 29, 1893, died October 25, 1977, and cremated at Woodend Crematorium, Aberdeen. He was also grandson of Prince John (Hanton), born 1861 and died December 27, 1942, and buried at Strathdon churchyard (Bellabeg).

Jack never was a serious man, he was always joking and fooling around and had a wicked sense of humor. For years he kept the secret of the prince (his grandfather) to himself. Jack would have been twenty when Prince John died, and as they were a very close family, the secret was kept untold.

Jack has two sons and he would call them "F" and "A", "F" being the eldest born in 1943 and "A" born in 1947; both are aware of the story or at least parts of their history. While doing our research (October 9, 2007), we found that Jack is still living in Forres, a town in northeast Scotland. When visited, Jack talked in riddles, but most had made sense. He touched on being a child/adult having to struggle, having to help the prince and old Jock work the crofts, and likewise listening to their stories round the peat fire.

Jack denied all knowledge of the stories to start with, but soon realized that the truth was already known. He verified the tales of his father, Old Jock, to a point and finished with a chilling fact by saying, "There is only one difference between me and the rest of them. They have all the money and I haven't any." He was making reference to the Royal Family within this statement, which he didn't say with anger, but quite matter of factly, with a touch of disappointment—disappointment in being lost and forgotten, which has swept through all the knowing family.

When taking leave of Jack, in his funny way and Doric voice he said, "Well, well, you ken far he's buried and that should be enough, so his loyalty and secrecy remains yet to this day very strong." Now what are they afraid of in this day and age … freedom?

Francis Hanton
Aunt of My Wife, Sheena

Francis Isabella Hanton was born May 15, 1936; she is the daughter of Old Jock Hanton and is still living in a residential home in Tarland (October 9, 2007). All her life, she has been a very outspoken woman and raised a family of five.

When we contacted her by phone and later by a visitation also, she was very willing to talk to us. We asked her why her mother and father were cremated instead of being entered beside Prince John and his wife (Jock's mother and father) at Strathdon, where he already had a layer. The truth came out—according to the family, they didn't want anyone snooping around the graves and delving into the past.

We are further down the line in a new and young generation who are living in a different time and want to trace their ancestors, and also with a strange sense of belonging and need to know.

In George Hanton's will, two bibles were left to George Hanton Jr. and a trunk left to Prince John. Somehow Prince John received all three and Francis wasted no time in telling us that her brother Jack had them. Jack denied all knowledge of them, but later when visiting his son "A," he informed us that he had the two bibles in a cupboard, but didn't know about the trunk. So, is this the men of the family trying to hide things again, and a vindictive woman throwing the story into the open because she didn't receive a bible? What was in the trunk? Was it as rumored that some of John Brown's possessions to be handed to his son? Where is it now? The search goes on.

Sheena Mary Cowe

Sheena May Cowe was born on January 22, 1948 and died February 16, 1987 (at the age of thirty-nine). She was the daughter of Mary H. Hanton, who married Charles Cowe, meaning that she was the granddaughter of Old Jock Hanton and great-granddaughter of Prince John. Sheena was my wife and bore me two fine sons named Michael and William.

In order that the Hantons were to keep their family history alive, Sheena, who was assisted by her mother and other Hanton family members, put together a family tree and some twenty years later, it was made into research, which made filling in the gaps to this story all the more interesting and easier.

The family tree dates back from John Brown to this present day. It gives a pretty good idea of where the Hantons fit in with the Leys and how an important role was played out between the Leys, Browns, and Hantons. I hope that anyone doing further research finds this family history and tree useful.

In her childhood, there remains a light-hearted story, which adds a little nicety between the families discussed.

Sheena, in her school years, helped the family by taking on part-time jobs when available. One such opportunity was as a beater on the glorious August 12 onward during the shooting season for red grouse and to a lesser extent ptarmigan. This starts as one of the busiest shooting days of the season with historically great volumes of game being shot. It serves as a boost to rural and local economies where moorland is predominant. This date differs for game other than the above stated, with most starting on

September 1 and October 1 being the opening day for woodcock and the predominant pheasant. UK laws /gaming law of 1831 had respect for not opening the shooting seasons on a Sunday, so in some years, it may be delayed until the August 13, and so on.

This job was referred to as "beating." Beating is an essential part of any successful shoot. If you are unfamiliar with what beating actually is, basically a beater is a person who has the job of flushing birds such as pheasants or grouse from cover in the direction of the guns. Beaters work as part of a team, normally led by the gamekeeper, moving through woodland or other cover such as heather and moorland to make sure that the birds fly in the desired direction, flushing the birds out using a stick.

Another aspect of beating is "flagging." This involves standing in areas where the birds are likely to flush and waving a colored flag, making loud noises, and flapping around to make the birds fly higher so they are a more challenging and exciting shot for the guns. Dogs can also be used in the beating line. These dogs need to be steady and under full control, so that the birds are flushed as the keeper desires. Dogs that are usually found in the beating line include spaniels and labradors, but all kinds of dogs have been trained for the role.

Anyway, it was getting windy and that area of moorland shoot had been covered, so the guns stood down and everyone was heading back toward the Land Rovers to move on to the next line. Sheena had her head down to shield her face from the wind, but also to ensure her footing as she ran down toward the awaiting vehicles. She rounded the back of one Land Rover and ran smack into one of the gentry's shooters. Well, as we say in this story, "He landed right on his arse."

Well, obviously Sheena was very apologetic as the man picked himself up, shook himself down, and stood to face her with a little smile about his face. He laughed amongst his fellow gentry, gave her a cuddle, and ensured her it was fine and all was well with no harm done. This fine tempered gentleman was no other than our current Queen's husband, Prince Philip. The funny thing is, that she knew him immediately as you would expect, but he had no idea that he had just met the great granddaughter of the "hidden prince."

At One Particular Shoot for Grouse

The John Brown Statue

It was the standing of John Brown in Deeside that the local people liked and respected. Most of the time he remained a man of mystery and it was not until after his death did a range of stories and myths appear. They sprang to life like a rabbit out of a hat, his power over the Queen and more, as most of the family was supposed to have obtained jobs through his influence.

Some rumors say that John Brown's wealth came from devious schemes and deals at the Royals' expense. Yes, he had money, but he was a very good benefactor to many local people in Ballater, Windsor, Crathie, and Braemar. At one time, he was accused of taking bribes from the local tradesman and shopkeepers. For decades John Brown's name has been assailed by common gossip and no allegations have ever been substantiated.

John Brown was indeed a clever man and possessed philosophy, which pleased the Queen and very much amused her. The fact that the rumours of a child being born to John Brown and Queen Victoria was rife, the closest anyone could get to the truth was an article written in the *Sunday People* in 1970. This article stated that a Dr. MacDonald (past curator of the Museum of Scottish Tartan in Comrie, Perthshire) was the first to mention the Queen bearing a child to John Brown.

My late wife, Sheena, and I tried to trace him, but all doors were shut and bolted as if Dr. MacDonald didn't exist.

John Brown's body rested in state until a handsome state coffin was constructed of polished oak and lead lined. At his funeral in Crathie Cemetery (April 5), other than the men standing in the community there was the guard of Hoaxar from Colonel Farquharson's men and the Earl of Fife's retainer from Marlodge. The coffin was draped with a worn plaid; this was done on the Queen's instructions as John Brown had often wrapped her in the plaid when they were out on many jaunts and excursions. The flowers on the graveside were legion, linking the paths and spilling into other graves.

Famed on Deeside, John Brown was well thought of, especially for his straight-forwardness and was never posh, nor put on airs, nor graces for anyone. When at Deeside, the Queen would frequent John Brown's graveside and her explicit instructions were to erect a gravestone similar to the one John Brown had erected for his parents, who are side-by-side.

The largest memorial to John Brown was a life-sized bronze statue the Queen had commissioned from Edgar Boehm, which was erected near the garden cottage at Balmoral Estate. The statue shows John Brown in highland dress with the Queen's medals on his left lapel; he also has his lucky three pence piece and pipe on his fob. The man's respectability doesn't finish there; on the Queen's death, King Edward VII ordered the statue to be hidden on the northeast side of a hill called Craig Gowan. It still remains there to this day.

If you the reader get the opportunity to visit the statue stay a while, and observe what John Brown is looking at, is he still observing Balmoral, his grave, Crathie village or the manse? Has the tradesman made sure he has the last laugh over those who detested and hated John Brown, or is it just the locals who are laughing with John and helping him to still reign supreme? After all, he did marry Queen Victoria and had a son. Is it fitting to call John Brown "King John" and his son "Prince John" or have they yet another unsolved riddle? Are they two people crying out to tell the world about their love, but the bureaucrats of the day being too bloody minded to allow it to happen?

There have been many John Brown enthusiasts who have frowned on the memorial statue being moved from its original place of pride at Balmoral Castle to its new location away out of sight, on the other side of a hill, and in amongst the trees.

It must be clarified that there must have been a lot of thought put into the new location and a mark of great respect from the Royal Family that he stands tall where he is.

If you stand beside the statue and look out over the Glen at what can be viewed, you will find the following main points of interest:

- Where John Brown was born.
- Where John Brown was raised.
- Where John Brown's family lived.
- Where John Brown was married.
- Where John Brown had a place of worship.
- Where John Brown was put to his final resting place among his family members.

The Stair Window of Crathie Manse

The manse at Crathie has various odd features, not only architectural, but superficial. When you enter the Crathie graveyard, which is immediately behind the manse, you will observe its unusually high wall, and if you do your homework correctly, you will find out that all that are entered there are related to one another.

The cemetery is a quiet, rough patch of ground and rather uneven, but there is one place an observer can view the Brown's graves, and that is from the first landing window on the stairs in the manse, which is situated on the back wall. The Queen on her frequent visits to John Brown's grave, liked privacy to pray, talk, and have comfort with him away from prying eyes and onlookers.

The manse window is exactly the same today as it was back then, except for the panes of frosted glass windows, but on one visit, the Queen made notice that the tradesmen were changing the glass pane and she ordered them to stop what they were doing. It was later discovered that staff of the manse and visitors wanted to watch Queen Victoria in the graveyard and spy on her solitude. An observer can look at the bottom panes in the windows and see they have been replaced, but do not allow you to see into John Brown's gravesite, as if you bend down to look out the window, the wall blocks your view. It is by royal command that the window must not be changed and only frosted glass is to be used.

Every time I have visited John Brown's grave, it has always supported a small bouquet of flowers. This is one line of enquiry we won't be taking and whoever puts them there, the family thanks you.

Standing at John Brown's grave, you can see that the top six panes of glass of the manse window are frosted to obscure the vision of nosey onlookers. Queen Victoria spent a lot of time mourning here and to this day, they remain frosted by royal command.

"Friend more than Servant, Loyal, Truthful, Brave, Self-less than Duty, even to the Grave."

Hanton Profile
Family Members

Doing some relaxed visiting and research of the Hanton family, we came across a wedding photo of my late wife's cousin's marriage and standing beside him in all her finery was Mary Ann Hanton (grandmother). She was Prince John's daughter and granddaughter to Queen Victoria and John Brown. She was born August 30, 1896 and died September 16, 1984 (aged eighty-eight). Her sister Molly (Sheena's mother) also bore a resemblance.

On showing the photo to my researchers, they were shocked at the similarities between Mary Ann and her grandmother. We, yet again, ask the question … How many other people have photos and other keepsakes that may have been handed down over the years and then later disregarded when the real story is dissuaded and forgotten? There are other members of the family that have also great similarities to the famous couple. A good swipe of John Brown himself and of Mrs. Brown, not only in looks, but in temperament also.

There are many photographs, which we have decided not to share at this point in order to give some protection to the families involved, but there is nothing more definite than what we have on file. You do not need a DNA test to show, in some cases, a spitting image, and in others a likeness you could not deny unless you were a fool.

Good stock for sure, but no knowledge of the facts other than certain family members, mostly the men folk.

The foundations and houses of Ballater are a good place to start to look for other potential relations. You will notice some houses were not built to house common folk.

It's worth a visit to the Royal train station in Ballater. You may see a familiar-looking face, as happened to one relation in our research. We popped in the visitors centre cafe for tea and scones and one of the waitresses kept staring at him. She eventually approached and asked him if he was "Royalty" by one of the staff. He replied no to uncomplicate matters and the reply came back, "Are you definitely sure?" An interesting conversation, although slightly embarrassing. Maybe a trip to the local post office may uncover some interesting facts?

It is a true fact of who do you think you are? And who are other people? Especially, in and around the Glen.

Watch and Chain Masonic
Modern Day Technology

I was to get a call with an invite to view an artefact and am a little skeptical about people phoning with invitations, but as it was a family member, I felt more than obliged to go and visit. I will call this family member "W" for privacy reasons.

"W" had a watch and chain that belonged to his father and the story goes this chain once belonged to John Brown. As I was able to borrow and inspect it, it proved to be stamped silver and the age would be about right. (There's a watch winder on the chain and silver Masonic square and compass.) During my research, I am finding that family members are opening up with more stories and tend to be more curious of what we have uncovered and put together, such as unearthing things like photos and stories that help us put the Hanton family history together and also help people to understand more about their own heritage.

What better background could a royal child get than to be brought up with the background of the Knights Templar from around 1187, then succeeded by the Hospitallers, or Knights of St. John of Jerusalem, and up to today the practice of Freemasonry which still has a large following, with a lodge at Pannanich and later a Masonic hall was built, which is now the Loirston Garden's and car park.

These organizations swore elegancy to crown and country, so in John Hanton's days, he would have been surrounded by just upright men who would have rather helped than hinder him.

The Headstone

The grandchildren of Prince John Hanton talked in riddles when questioned where he and his wife were, whether this was deliberate or an effect of old age, we don't know. We were not daunted by this, as a few short phone calls to various parish registrars gave us the answer.

There is a small village in Aberdeenshire named Bella Beg (area where the Lonach march takes place) and there on the side of the hill overlooking the village is an old historic church with two graveyards, armed with a copy of the numbered entries and grave numbers we visited in the graveyards.

It was as if we were attracted by a magnet; my researcher and I did not require any guidance or maps, as we were drawn straight to the graveside. The stone was covered in moss, which we duly scraped off in order to read the inscription. With a cross reference with the parish registrar, we had proved beyond a doubt that we had found the lost prince's grave and, by fate, lying almost back to back was the grave of my late wife's parents (Mary Hanton and Charles Cowe).

Having done all that, we then decided to do a small research on the religious side of Prince John; having being brought up with a good education, he toiled as a road foreman before retiring to the small carrier's croft at Alford. Church records tell us that he never missed a Sunday service and was indeed a member of the Church of Scotland. It would have been very nice to see Prince John and his son Auld Jock and their wives dressed in their finery walking down the road to the church.

Such was the Hanton family's devotion to religion that on the bottom of Prince John's headstone are the words, "He giveth his beloved sleep." At first, we thought nothing of it and then it started niggling at the back of our minds. We had to research it.

> Elizabeth Barret Browning 1806-1861
> "What would we give to our beloved?
> The hero's heart to be unmoved,
> The poet's star-tun'd harp, to sweep,
> The patriot's voice, to teach and rouse,
> **The monarch's crown, to light the brows?**
> 'He giveth His beloved sleep.'"

The Resting Place of John Hanton

Pananich or Pannanich?

Our search for Broom Cottage, Pannanich, was a long one and very frustrating, but a cup of coffee with an old friend in Aberdeen had me on the trail again.

Margaret Leys, spinster, states in her will (June 22, 1897) that she had a house at Kintore Crathie and also lived at Broom Cottage, Pannanich. Margaret worked as a domestic servant and never married.

George Hanton and his wife, Mary Leys (Margaret's sister), had a house at Newton Grange, Crathie and also lived at Broom Cottage, Pannanich. They employed a domestic servant and Mary died May 10, 1916.

The proper address would be:

> Broom Cottage, Pannanich Village
> United Parishes
> Glenmuick Tuloch
> Glencairn

This is all part of Pannanich village estate; the Hanton family lived in one with boy John and his aunt Margaret Leys lived in another one. The other tenants are not known and neither are the owners of the houses, but according to the map of Ballater and Strathdon and by the ordinance survey and various old maps of Pannanich, we have the main road going right passed the door of the Pannanich Hotel and listed clearly by the row of houses in front, commanding a lovely view is Pannanich Lodge.

So armed with two people we invited who are descendants of Prince John, they led us to Broom Cottage and took us to a door in the Pannanich Lodge, so local knowledge and local maps gave us the information we required. The four houses in a row standing in front of Pannanich Hotel/Inn started life as a stately lodge and, as time went by, they were latterly called Broom Cottage; I believe they are all part of the hotel complex now. It has to be stated that all the time the Hantons and Leys lived at Broom Cottage, it belonged to a titled person and they had life tenure free of charge.

Further to our enquiries, the records of the Masonic Lodge St. Nathalan of Tulloch in Mar Ballater No. 259 when founded in 1815, held the following information:

> William Clerk – Treasurer … lived at Pannanich Lodge.
> James McHardy "Wright" - Past Master … lived at Pannanich Lodge.
> John Stewart - Past Master … lived at Pannanich Lodge.

This gives us more documented proof that Pannanich Lodge was a row of houses with people of various backgrounds living in them.

The original site of the above-mentioned lodge is also known. We must remember that Pannanich village and community existed long before Ballater turned into the bustling village it was this day. Pannanich Inn was the only coaching inn in the area with livery for horses. It supported a spa and its waters were well known; there was work in the area with farming, forestry, and road building, and it also supported a ferry over the River Dee. There was also a crofting community there and a small shop, which used a barter system.

In the early days, the settlers were people who were like the Browns, changing their names in order to survive and the harsh life the clan system brought. Sadly, the community does not exist anymore and all but a few houses have disappeared and people have moved on. Our research in that area showed only a few people are local and most of them are not aware of the local history. On visiting Pannanich Inn, I was met by a lady in 1800s period costume and also came across a young boy with bare feet and a begging bowl at different times. Both had lovely smiles and a comforting manner, but they disappeared as silently and as quickly as they came. I was left with a question in my mind … these meetings were in broad daylight … could I have met Margaret Leys? But, who was the boy? Whoever they were, they were both happy.

Ballater

The land that Ballater is situated on once belonged to Farquharson of Inverey, but James, the last laird, exchanged the property with the Farquharsons of Monaltrie who at the time were based at Crathie. This move gave James his dream of owning land on Donside.

During the 1745 Jacobite uprising, Farquharson raised troops for Prince Charlie, but was later captured at Culloden and exiled to England for approximately forty years.

Elspeth Michie had been bathing and drinking water from the Pannanich Wells and was said to have a miracle cure from scrofula or tuberculosis of the lymph nodes from the spa waters. Farquharson returned from exile and developed the spa. Visitors flocked to Pannanich, but they required accommodation and the only suitable land to build on was on the opposite side of the river.

Farquharson granted feus for the land in Ballater to be built on, and the area was known locally as Sluivannachie. It was covered by heather and broom and droves of cattle rested there on their way south to market. If it wasn't for the Pannanich wells and spa, Ballater would not have existed.

This development created a fair amount of work in the area and a young John Brown had a job as an ostler at Pannanich stables at first. Ballater, far from the maddening crowds, was just a little village, but it started to build and expand when Victoria and Albert bought Balmoral. The arrival of the railway in 1861 saw the start of Balmoral's growth. It went from 271 residents to a population of 1,256 people in 1901. Now it attracts visitors from all over the world and every corner of Britain. It is said that the larger houses were built in the town for royal offspring born on the wrong side of the bed, so to speak.

Our Family Bibles

On obtaining a copy of the will of George Hanton of Broom Cottage, Pannanich, we discovered that he left a large trunk to John Hanton (his son) and to young George he left two family bibles known as the "Scots Bibles." How the Scots Bibles came to be in this branch of the family, we don't know. What we do know is that John ended up with them and when he died, he left them to Old Jock (his son) and then on his death, it was passed to Jack Hanton (his son), who is now still alive and living in Forres. Now Jack Hanton has passed them to his son "A," who also lives in Forres.

My researcher was allowed to take a photo of them and they are both in excellent condition—one has John Hanton's wedding recorded inside and is signed by the minister and the other remains blank.

With the barriers and secrecy broken down, we were shown a mantle clock that still keeps good time to this day. This clock was presented to John Hanton and his wife for their service to the community of Alford.

We then tried to trace the travelling trunk and, once again, we found a little hatred or jealousy in the family, but we discovered it was still held within the family.

The family bibles that contain the story and written in the prince's own hand.

John Brown's Parents

Father John Brown leased Crathienaird property called Bridge of Bush; he was a schoolmaster turned farmer. John Brown's mother (Mary Leys) was the daughter of an abrader blacksmith.

We must remember that after the Jacobite uprising in 1745, the clan system was a mess as some were facing extinction and deportation to other lands. Murder was rife so the Lamont's that had land in southwest Scotland very cleverly changed their names to Brown, Black, and White in order to survive in Scotland.

John Brown's kinfolk came and settled in Deeside in a valley that was quiet and peaceful, and they managed to scrape a healthy living any way they could, although John Jr. was born at Bridgend five years later, they all moved to Bush Farm.

We must remember that history tells us that the Lamont men were all tall strong men and not afraid of a day's work, but all of them were very well taught and able to read and write, conversing in English and Gaelic. The Brown family went to local schools, but much of their education came from their father while sitting round the peat fire during the evenings.

Books were scarce in those days and most of the reading was done from the family bible; most of the teachings came from there, as well. Being in the Glen and as tranquil as it was, they were living hand in hand with nature itself, plenty of wild herbs for cooking and medical potions, and an abundance of salmon, deer, and other wildlife. Eggs from most birds were used for cooking and baking. Birds like lapwing, pigeon, pheasant, grouse, and seagull were treated like a great delicacy. Bread and cheese you got from a barter system with your neighbor or from any small shop in the area.

The Family Tree at a Glance
John and Victoria Brown
&
Prince John (Hanton)

George Hanton	(1837-1920)	The Given Parentage
Mary Leys	(1834-1916)	

Family of Above

John Hanton	(1861-1942)	John Brown - Queen Victoria - Son John
George Hanton	(1864-1949)	
William Hanton	(1869-1909)	
Francis Hanton	(1873-1953)	

John Hanton married Mary Ann Anderson in 1892.

George Hanton	(1892-1892)
John Hanton	(1893-1977)
Helen Hanton	(1895-1954)
Mary Ann Hanton	(1896-1984)
Alexander Hanton	(1901-1992)
Eliza Jane Hanton	(1904-1990)
Isabella Hanton	(1907-1992)

Marriages of Above

Mary Ann Hanton - Charles Middleton	(1915)
Helen Hanton - George Ritchie	(1932)

John Hanton - Eliza Jane Newlands   (1921)
Eliza Hanton - Reginald Foulsham   (1933)
Isabella Hanton - Jack Panting   (1936)
Alexander Hanton - Margaret Scotpryd   (1942)

Family of John Hanton and Eliza Jane Newlands
William John Hanton   (1922)
Mary Helen Hanton   (1925-1994)
Frances Isabella Hanton   (1936)
Margaret Eliza Hanton   (1938-1994)

Marriages of Above
William Hanton - Katherine Coutts   (1943)
Mary Hanton - Charles Cowe   (1947)
Francis Hanton - George Crawford   (1955)
Margaret Hanton - Peter Hutcheson   (1965)

Family of Mary H. Hanton and Charles Cowe
Sheena Mary Cowe   (1948-1987)
Charles John Cowe   (1949)
Bruce Alexander Cowe   (1950-1952)
Margaret Isabella Cowe   (1954)
Edith Jane Cowe   (1960)

Marriages of Above
Sheena Mary Cowe - William Milne Rennie   (1969)
Charles John Cowe - Amy Ogston   (1971)
Margaret Isabella Cowe - Frank Reid   (1989)
Edith Jane Cowe - Hugh Costie   (1981)

Family of Sheena Mary Cowe and William Milne Rennie
William Milne Rennie   (1969)
Michael Charles Rennie   (1970)

At the time of putting the family tree together, we did not include all family members, as it is hoped you will appreciate, it could become a little tedious, confusing, and boring. I have tried to show the direct line all the way down through the ages to my two sons (William and Michael).

Further researchers will be able to trace their family lines from what has been researched and recorded here and I wish them the best of luck. At this time, my research is still ongoing, as I feel there are more facts and stories to be revealed.

Another piece of the family tree states that John Brown and Francis Clark (cousins, both having served for the queen) were nephews of Mary and Margaret Leys. Although the two women were of similar age, they were indeed the boys' aunts.

On researching Auld Jock's stories told to Sheena and I all those years ago, it was found that the stories and references were all interwoven with one another and tie in beautifully at certain stages. Each giving the other a cross reference, family members with old letters that haven't seen the light of day in generations all hold stories about one person or another, revealing their habits, clothes of the period, and family history, which is very fascinating. Days and people gone by, times that we can only read about and only then if we believe the harshness, cruelty, and narrow-mindedness that existed then.

If today's life is to be expected and a comparison made of two hundred years ago, then I am all for life today and the luxuries that go with the present; we are warm, clean, well fed, and live in a caring community. I am old fashioned in values as, well, but like most of us we live for freedom and our country, Scotland.

Proof
The Story So Far

John Brown's mother was a Leys and she had two late sisters of similar age to John Brown, which makes them aunts to John Brown. The confidante of Queen Victoria and boss of the family was John Brown's mother.

George Hanton and Mary Leys were married just before John was born, John being called after his father (John Brown) and used the adopted name of Hanton. This was so John and his supposed three brothers George, William, and Francis were brought up as John Brown's cousins, making it relatively easy for John Brown to visit the boy.

All of this we have documentary proof of and some of the family are well versed in the story of cousin John Brown, but we must remember that the Dee Side Glen was a close knit community and the truth was well known. One reason for the secrecy was that the royal household was the largest employer in the Glen and the locals respected that.

The Royals also brought sightseers and the early form of tourist, as well as opening up the Glen with better roads and a rail service. So, the boy's identity was well hidden as none in the Glen would mention him, but full marks to my researchers for helping me unravel so many cryptic clues. This is a part of history that was well hidden one hundred and fifty years ago, but it is a story that is well told and never forgotten.

Let's look at the bloodline from another angle; as yet, we have no royal proof other than family stories that Queen Victoria was mother to John Hanton. Let's look at today's technology such as DNA.

(To be completed if Royal samples are made available and the test types allow in the future.)

The Throne

The man that lay quiet and is the legitimate son of Queen Victoria he being now deceased, was well informed of his background. Call it what you will. John Hanton (Scottish/Aberdonian) made sure that the family knew their history and it has been handed down through all the generations.

John Brown, who was Queen Victoria's devoted servant, lover, and husband had an ill-fated time, but only secrecy could keep them together and coupled with undying devotion to each other.

Our attempts to access Queen Victoria's will have resulted in failure. We were able to find that there were special orders given to seal all documents and not make them available to the authorities or the general public. On February 9, 2008, an article in the local newspaper (*The Press and Journal*) stated that another royal case of a 53-year-old possible descendant/offspring has won his case, where the Lord Chief of Justice (Lord Phillips) ruled that this person was entitled to a hearing of his case and to inspect the wills.

It has been seen and recorded as vexatious and an abuse of process. The man's name is Mr. Brown from Jersey. He apparently told the hearing, "This appeal raises important questions as to the circumstances in which wills, in particular these of members of the Royal Family, can be sealed and hidden from public inspection and the circumstances in which wills have been sealed can be unsealed."

So this throws new light on all the stories that we have been told over the years, stories about other offspring from other Royals. It certainly makes you wonder. While this book is in compilation and even with the research that has been done, in relation to the Hanton family … who are the true Royals? How many are there? You go to work and who is the person next to you?

Male or female, do they all know their ancestry? Who was the tramp on the road? Or, the people who lived next door? What was the postman's background? They all won't have big houses, posh cars, or 4x4s. They may never have been on horseback or gone shooting in their lives, but they may have royal blood.

Forget the Royals that we see on the television and read about it in the papers, take them out of the equation, and let us take a good look. Who is it that should really be sitting on the throne? It shows us that through the ages men and women are alike; no matter their standing in the community, they all enjoy sex and a bit of flirtation.

So let us get back to John Brown and Queen Victoria. The so-called rumourmongers and muckslingers weren't about to get away with their stories, as most of the rumours were true and none of us in Scotland gave a damn. We just let them get on with their very own private life.

Muckslinging in royal circles has been going on for years—"Let's take a cruise until things die down a bit."

"Let's put someone else in the limelight until the story takes a back seat."

The politics go on and on and I'm sure you, the reader, can come up with some interesting stories and facts yourself. We humble peasants can only look on and smile and thank God that we can go about our business without paparazzi, or have a good scratch at out private parts without someone taking a few snapshots and selling them to newspapers worldwide.

What price can you put on freedom?

Queen Victoria's Grief Revealed in Letters

Quoted from the *Press and Journal* (February 11, 2008), "Handwritten letters have come to light which reveal Queen Victoria's grief following the death of her most trusted highland servant John Brown."

The documents written by the Queen at Balmoral and Windsor Castle during the 1880s were sent to Lilly Wellesley, the wife of her personal chaplain. In them she speaks of her personal grief at the death of John Brown, who was a gillie from Crathie who went to work at Balmoral Castle when Victoria and Albert bought it in 1853.

Following the death of her husband in 1861, Mr. Brown became the Queens's personal attendant and rumors of an improper relationship circulated. At the time, those were dismissed by Victoria as ill-natured gossip and this, to us, was nothing the family didn't already know. The article went on to say:

"The letters offered for sale by Canadian bookseller/dealer Lois Caron, reveal the loss felt by the Queen following Mr. Brown's death at Windsor in February 1883 aged fifty-six years. On March 27, 1883 she wrote, 'I am sorely stricken as he was so strong and powerful and his health and constitution so remarkably strong.' She also wrote, "I felt as sure as one can be of anything human that he would be longley preserved to me."

In later letters, she talks about pilgrimages visiting his grave, "Yes, bygone days were bright and happy and now seems to me that life is without light." One letter goes on to say, "One goes on - There may be gleams - but there is a dead weight, a heaviness from which you must rouse yourself," as she wrote from a visit to Crathie Church.

The collection of fifteen letters expected to collect around 10,000 pounds also expressed words of comfort sent by the Queen to Mrs. Wellesley on the death of her husband in 1882 and the son whom Victoria had been godmother to less than a year later.

There is more in the article, but these are the only parts that we feel are pertinent to the Hanton story; yes, even today people are curious of Victoria's relationship with John Brown. They all want to be part of it and they, in general, want to find out the truth.

Perhaps it might even be better if we don't conclude this story and leave the conclusion for a later date, keeping you in suspense for a few years, yet, but I won't, as my researchers and I feel it is only fit and proper that we tell the complete story as it has been handed down to us and especially with the renewed interest from the media.

Perhaps with the publication of our story and history of the Hanton family, people in general will learn and maybe someone somewhere can tie up any loose ends that we have left dangling and once again rekindle a renewed interest in what is to us a fascinating story and heritage.

The worst that could happen would be the powers that be would want to silence my researchers and me. Would they try to prosecute me for keeping alive an old man's historic tale of history and heritage? Let's be realistic … what possible harm would it do in today's society to let the public know the truth, especially when, thanks to the media among others, we already know plenty of scandal from past and present Royals circles1}.

Will they try to silence me as they did back in 1985 with Dr. Michael MacDonald and his story? It was stated that Dr. MacDonald could have gone to the tower with his statements that Victoria and Brown were married and that she bore him a son. What will happen to me? Do you think I will be decapitated and my head mounted on a fence stake on the entrance to the small Aberdeenshire village of Stuartfield, or will they simply quiet me by giving me a couple days fishing on the River Dee?

I really think that I will quietly publish this small book of family history and brave the storms that come after. Someone someday will discover everything that we have and open up a new family history supporting this one because we, as you have already read, have been sworn to secrecy of certain locations and artefacts.

What will happen if the hiding place of John Brown and Queen Victoria's marriage were to be suddenly and accidentally discovered and exposed, or some smart alec architect discover the extensions that were erected to a rather unassuming building, extending its frontage to give a rather commanding view over the River Dee.

The guests were able to stroll on the small secluded lawns sheltered by trees and away from prying eyes, and nosey busy bodies would think nothing of a family party on a Sunday afternoon, or a group of friends just relaxing on the Lord's Day after attending church—a close community unwittingly setting the trail for a long investigation starting one hundred and thirty years ago and leaving cryptic clues all over the place.

How I feel for Mr. and Mrs. Brown who were bogged down by bureaucrats and other small-minded people, that they were not allowed to be themselves unless it was behind closed doors; they wanted to shout at the world and declare their romance and total devotion to each other. I take my hat off to them, especially under the difficult times they lived in and the things they had to put up with. John Brown was right in his quotation, "It's nothing but cald kale."

The Leys Family

We have researched the Brown family and their origins from southwest Scotland and their cheiftainship of the Lamonts, but what about John Brown's mother and aunts who brought up and educated the young prince.

The Leys family had extensive lands around Banchory, but during the inter- feudal clan systems that existed back in those days, the lands of Leys was taken from them and granted to the Burnett family in 1323 by King Robert the Bruce. If you, by chance, get to visit Crathie's Castle, which is situated just outside Banchory in the heart of Royal Deeside, look out for the jewelled ivory ancient horn of Leys in the great hall. This item was given to the family to mark his generous gift.

It is very interesting to note that the building of the Crathie's Castle did not begin until 1553, almost two hundred and thirty years after the Leys were robbed and pushed off their lands. It is also interesting to note that the Leys Clan came under the flag of the McPherson's Clan, who were renowned musicians and shrewd businesspeople.

In the delay of building the castle, is it possible that the Burnett family was afraid of repercussions from the Leys and McPhersons, because fortunes and lands changed hands at regular intervals in those days, or was this the drawing to a close of the historical clan battles and the beginning of a new way of life?

Considering the facts of what the politicians of the day had to say about John Brown and Queen Victoria, is it a fact that the Queen had a loyal servant who had chief blood in his veins from both sides of his family and could stand proud and tall amongst them all. Therefore, it is to our belief that when Queen Victoria and John Brown married, they were on equal terms and standing. The Queen did not marry a lowly servant, but rather a fiercely proud clansman with a loyalty to his Queen.

This is the Horn of Leys, which is prominently displayed in a case over the fireplace in the Great Hall. Family tradition has it that the Horn of Leys was given by Robert the Bruce in 1323.

Cousin John Brown

Most interesting to find, is that all the Leys and Hanton family descendants refer to John Brown as cousin, and only the direct relatives and secret holders would whisper the name in its true magnitude.

Yes, John Brown was a nephew to his mother's younger sisters Margaret and Mary Leys, and when his aunt Mary married George Hanton, this would have made him a cousin to the Hanton family children … all except John Hanton, who was John Brown and Queen Victoria's son, cleverly hidden and brought up as the eldest son of the Hantons.

Throughout all the records and documents we have, they all show that George Hanton Jr. was the eldest son and treated so, but George Hanton and his wife, Mary, treated all the children including young John Hanton as equals. From an early age, they were very well educated and were understanding of their chores around the house and croft.

Living hand and nature gave them a good upbringing. To this day, the older people in the Glen try to avoid talking about "the child," whether it was to be kept part of the family history or laid open for the world to see. I don't know, only time will tell.

Having met some Brown families during our investigation, we have been told many stories. An elderly man told us that when the family was being discussed, he was always forbidden to stay and hear the conversation and had to sit outside in the garden. Another man had told us of two members of the Brown clan, trying to find out about John Brown and Queen Victoria so they could record the history of the affair, but some years apart both men died suddenly without completion of their findings.

It was promised to all the people that have taken part in collating this history that the truth as projected shall be made public so the "hidden" may rest in peace.

John Brown's CV at a Glance

Date of birth December 8, 1826, at Crathienaird, Crathieparish, Aberdeenshire. He was educated at Crathie Parish School (his father was head master), he could speak fluent English and Gaelic, and was able to read and write. He was taught religious studies and calligraphy lessons from his parents, he left school at an early age, and was employed as an ostler's assistant and an innkeeper's assistant at Pannanich Inn. While working there, he shared a small room with other servants. This accommodation can be found at the east end of the front row of five houses, which is sometimes known as Pannanich Lodge or Broom Cottage. In today's terms, the accommodations looked like nothing more than a coal shed; inside the stout robust walls there is little room to live or sleep.

Some time later, he worked as a part-time farm laborer and worked at the Glen when he could; he soon earned a name for himself as a hard worker. Eventually, at the age of sixteen years in 1842, he went to work as gillie and pony man for Robert Gordon on Balmoral Estate.

In 1848, the Royal Family took over Balmoral Estate and John at the age of twenty-two years, was retained in the same position. By 1851, John was in the permanent role of leader of the Queen's pony. In 1858, John found himself personal gillie to Prince Albert and then by 1864, John entered into permanent service to Queen Victoria and received two medals (the faithful servant's medal and the devoted servant's medal).

In all, it is quite an impressive CV of his life and many years will pass before the House of Windsor gives up any of its secrets and documents relating to John Brown, his beloved Queen, and their relationship.

We must bear in mind that in these times and location it was the start of a climate change of inter-clan warfare, military rule, and the progression to receive the first policeman in the Glen. The thought process of people toward stature and acceptable practices were indeed restricted and reserved during the Victorian era, although in reality it was definitely the opposite.

As he looked in more mature years in all his finery.

The residence of John Brown when he started working life as a stable boy.

Crathie Naird

For the birthplace of John Brown, most of the story is not documented and may never be recorded. If you go west through Crathie and look for the B939 on your right, take that turn, and travel up the hill, through the bends, and about one mile ahead is Crathie Naird on the left. If you look closely, there was a settlement or group of small crofts situated 1,200 feet above sea level, the ground was barren, rough, and the residents of the time barely scraped together an existence. The Browns were fortunate as John's father was a crofter, which ran concurrent with his abilities in educational and teaching skills.

John Brown stayed at Crathie Naird for approximately five years until the family moved to another settlement called Bridgend of Bush, which is less than a mile away in the same glen, but north of Crathie Naird. All the settled communities spoke Gaelic in these times with the Browns living at Braeneach, until John Brown's father died and his mother moved down to Newton Cottage, Crathie.

If you look at the early ordinance server map, you can clearly pinpoint both settlements north of the River Dee and Balmoral, which was easily accessible by way of pony and trap so you could visit the Glen, spend some time, and return in a day without rush.

Time has progressed now and both settlements have nearly disappeared under the plough with all that remains being two fair-sized farms with large fields. Both areas would have been sheltered by trees and the ground cleared of moss and heather. The stones cleared from the land were used to build walls for thatched houses and walls around the fields to protect and give shelter to the croft animals.

There is an outlook from today's travellers that would recall this type of area as "one of the most romantic settings with a commanding and panoramic view south down the glen" and looking for the most part snow capped, down the mountain off dark Loch Nagar, but life in those days was hard and far from romantic.

Crathie Manse

We mentioned this building some time ago, but let us take a closer look at it. At first glance, it appears normal and even from a side elevation it looks fairly normal. Stop and take a step back and really observe the true nature of the building. It looks as if two separate houses were stuck together as the older back building was built with stone and lime with the windows being small as per period setting and design. The front section of building is constructed of cement and good dressed stone. It is very cleverly done having two buildings built, but years apart. If you have a look closer at the front building, it is wider at both sides than the old building, which creates two fair-sized rooms with fairly high ceilings and large bay windows.

The hallway is fairly substantial with plenty of room to mingle and stretch one's legs after a long and tedious sermon often given by guest ministers, such as Reverend McLeod, which indicates that the Royals and their guests in the early days didn't attend Crathie Church, but sometimes attended service twice on Sundays at Crathie Manse.

Have a look at this building and its history, especially the entrance or porch as it serves to be more fitting for a plush resident and, although it's not out of place for any class of attendee, it would be unlikely on visitation to be given a second glance, or even turn the heads towards the frontage with its wooded lawn and the River Dee flowing by. Any guests to the manse could enjoy the tranquil setting with a feeling of peace and contentment, while in total privacy. You will experience the same tranquil romantic feeling if you take the time to visit and absorb.

How many mysteries does this building hold with distinguished guests such as Queen Victoria, Prince Albert, John Brown, various prime ministers, members of the government, and Royal visitors from other lands? If only the walls could talk, all the mysteries and secrets could be exposed.

The manse at Crathie showing the difference in gavel and constructions.

Showing the privacy Victoria received at Johns Brown's grave by way of having the top six panes of glass on the manse window frosted by royal decree.

John Brown - Intestate

Lodged with Sheriff Grimichie in Aberdeen was an inventory of John Brown's belongings.

Savings with the Union Bank of Scotland Ltd., Braemar

Banked £1000 October '82   + Interest of £20   Total - £1020
Banked £750 November '82   + Interest of £12   Total - £762

Banked with the North of Scotland Bank Ltd., Braemar

Banked £3100 November '82 + Interest £53   Total - £3153
Cash Found in Deceased Repositories   Total - £1185

Personal Items Pictures, Books, Jewelry, etc.

From Windsor Castle, Buckingham Palace, and
Osborn house.   Total - £208
Salary and Pension Due   Total - £101
Less Stamp Duty   Total - £207

In this day and age, it could be confirmed that the conversion from then 'til now in monetary value would be approximately four million pounds, approximated using the GDP per capita conversion system of monetary value.

There is no record of where the money went to and in dying in what is called intestate (with no will), one can only look at the monies being returned to the crown (his wife) or did Alexander profit Her Majesty's commissioner, A. F. Leslie, JP for the county of Banff and Sheriff Clark, deputy for Aberdeenshire, share out the money with the surviving siblings of Brown's family?

The Prince John Hanton didn't receive a penny, as there were no instructions of that nature found, but interestingly, there is some word that this document is also under "safe" keeping by Royal Order. It is interesting to note that on Hugh Brown's death, his will stated that he had left two thousand eight hundred and fifty-eight pounds eleven shillings and two pence. This would have worked out to approximately half his brother's wealth, and let's not forget that Hugh and John were indeed very close.

If indeed it was entrusted to go to the sibling by word of mouth, then that is where it stopped and someone other than the rightful recipient filled their pockets.

It is interesting to note that John Brown's salary in 1866 was £150 and in 1869 it rose to £230, his personal allowance for clothes was £70 and in 1872 John was designated Squire with a final salary of £400. This amount of money to be in the possession of servants is quite strange, don't you think? Within the concluded testimony of witness given by Her Majesty Queen Victoria, it is stated that the said John Brown had died with no offspring and that this was correct as "only answerable to God."

This statement is true, as being the Queen she was, as depicted in many royal documentaries, not to be answerable to any mortal person and only recognized God as a superior being to which she would stand accountable.

In holding the faith, it may be assumed that in her heart she felt that God would understand why she would deny her own child in the presence of others, forgive her, see it was for the protection of her Crown, all her family, and safe from the unwarranted persecution that would have been forthcoming if this information had leaked into the wrong, disrespectful hands. At this point, it is understandable why secrecy had to be kept and secured. These times she lived in were unforgiving, more so than today.

It would have been interesting if a will of John Brown's was found made prior to his death, if he would have left his son out of the equation. ... But, of course, he died prematurely.

John Brown's Birthplace – Crathie Naird

Let us take a closer look at the place called Crathie Naird. Crathie Naird is self-explanatory, as you have a village and parish called Crathie, and by using the old Gaelic and old Scotch you must remember that places were described as back to front sentences.

A translation for the word *"naird"* is found all over Scotland and generally used as the second half of a name; it doesn't tell you much if you don't have the Gaelic or the old Scotch, but *naird* itself is a sentence of desperation. In reality, it is describing where the place is as translation of *naird* is "close to or nearer to" and in this case it's Crathie nearer to—a bad English translation you may say, but in today's English it would read Near to Crathie. In the old language Naird Crathie, which is back to front, *Crathie* being the place and *Naird* being the descriptive word so that travellers and visitors in those times knew how to describe the place for which they were looking.

If you get out a map of Scotland and have a look at what you can find or how many names you can find ending in *naird*, start with Kinaird, the lighthouse in Fraserburgh, which started life as a castle. You will be surprised on the amount of *nairds* you will find. It's sad that the old language is no longer taught at schools, as this was suppressed in usage for the proper spoken English, and it is true that for many years classmates could be punished for using such language. It would be nice if it were revived and encouraged today before the dialect is lost forever from our spoken tongue.

The question must be raised that if we do nothing to save this part of local culture, will we be able to do accurate translations in the future, or will they be translating with a foreign enhancement, which will not be able to capture the true meanings as per the given dialect?

The last long house standing in the area and the birthplace of John Brown. The "black house" (Scottish Gaelic: *taigh dubh* (formerly "tigh") is a traditional type of house, which used to be common in Highland Scotland.

The buildings were generally built with double wall dry-stone walls packed with earth and wooden rafters covered with a thatch of turf with cereal straw or reed. The floor was generally flagstones or packed earth and there was a central hearth for the fire. There was no chimney for the smoke to escape, though. Instead, the smoke made its way through the roof.

The black house (long house) was used to accommodate livestock, as well as people. People lived at one end and the animals lived at the other with a partition between them.

After the wars of independence, which Scotland fought against England between 1296 and 1314, much of the land held by the pro-English was forfeited and later given to Scottish patriots. Land, thus, passed to a King's favorite was handed down to the next and successive generations.

The word "clan," meaning children (in Gaelic, *Clann*), was coined and in the future each member of a clan claimed kinship with his chief, who was looked upon as a land-owning aristocrat. Clansmen worked for their chief and fought for him in battle, and in return he administered justice and in his own way provided for the dependants of those who had given him good and faithful service.

Those who were good to their chief were even allowed to assume their chief's surname, if they so desired. The clansmen were "tenants at will" and could be moved from place to place, depending on the requirements of the chief. The clansmen or tenants worked on the land on a system known as *run-rig*. This meant that the inby land was allocated on a yearly basis, so that every tenant had to share in the bad land, as well as the better land.

William McCombie - Cattle Breeder

What has an Aberdeen Angus cattle breeder from Donside got to do with John Brown and Queen Victoria?

More than what is first recognized by many, there is a decisive link too prominent not to mention.

Mr. McCombie was a native of Tillyfourie near Alford in Aberdeenshire, born the son of a farmer and cattle dealer. He was well educated, but gave up his studies at Aberdeen University to work as a horseman on his father's farm.

Young McCombie dealt in cattle before becoming a tenant farmer in his own right in 1829. It was not long before he became a noted breeder of Aberdeen Angus cattle and, with good management of his livestock and planned mating, he was able to improve the breed and stock.

McCombie's successful breeding program saw him winning prizes from the Paris Exposition of 1878 to the Alford Cattle Show and onward. Queen Victoria often visited the herd at Tilly and enjoyed Aberdeen Angus beef, which was often delivered as a Christmas present. The meat was famed for its taste and redness with little fat.

It is noted that McCombie was recognized as the preserver of the Aberdeen Angus herd and was able to develop and strengthen it, and with recognition of his work, a statue was erected in 2001 by Prince Charles in the presence of Queen Elizabeth. Both, in their own right, noted the Aberdeenshire Angus breeder and gave recognition to his achievements. The statue is well located for viewing and can be found on the roadside just east of Alford.

Now, this is where the story gets really interesting. Why were many of McCombie's cattle called by the same names as Queen Victoria's racehorses? One such beast was a prize bull called John Hanton, no less.

Is this too much of a coincidence or is this a second attempt of creating mystery while attempting to tell the world the truth? It must be said again that Queen Victoria and John Brown wanted to shout out to the world and claim their true affections, but protocol and bureaucrats in that day would not allow them to do so, as the price for their devotion may have been the ruin of the Monarchy.

Ballater Church

Research often leads to many surprising things as my researcher, who was doing a "bang up" job on this subject, found himself a bit fed up, on a day when things were not going too well for him in Ballater. On walking up the street, he observed that the Ballater Church was open. On entering, he found a strange tranquil peace come over him as he relaxed in a pew.

Taking in the various names and plaques on the wall, he was somewhat aware that an elderly couple were coming toward him and, after a few preliminary words of introduction, they asked where he came from and what he was doing. On this area he was careful not to let any information slip out and politely told them he was doing research into his family tree and also mentioned a few names. The elderly couple looked at each other with caution and started to tell him a story almost identical to the one you have just read.

When they approached a parting of company, they shook hands and the elderly man said it was nice to see and meet a grandson of the Prince John.

Even to this day, the Glen residents are reluctant to speak or discuss the subject so their silence is to be respected and the elderly couple will remain anonymous to everyone. Today on the April 14, 2008, they are still alive and attend Ballater Church regularly.

It is wondered how many other people throughout the world are aware of this particular twist in historical Royal movements and would they dare come forward and tell the truth before this is long forgotten?

Crathie Church

There was a church there for a number of years, but it was rather neglected; a total restoration and rebuilding was started in 1893 with Queen Victoria laying the foundation stone and it was re-opened in 1895. The minister at the time was A. A. Campbell and these records can be confirmed with the church records that are on display inside the church.

These records confirm to us that the manse at Crathie, although extensively revamped prior to 1893, was used by the Royal Family as a place of worship with the guest higher Archie of the church conducting the service periodically, the main man of the cloth, in trust and favour by Victoria, being no other than the respected Reverend Norman MacLeod.

The refurbished Crathie Church as it looks today.

Rabb - The Sheep Farmer
The Chance Meeting

We had heard of a man who lived high upon a hill in the Glen just north of Balmoral Castle. "Approachability and acceptance may be a problem," was given as a prior warning, due to the fact that he had lived all his life with his late mother in a relatively secluded and sheltered lifestyle. He never married; he lived alone and shared his house with his animals. There was also prior warning of this local man talking in riddles, but mostly in a language no one knew and, interestingly, we were told he was the oldest original person in the Glen. All we had to go on was that he smoked continuously and that he only washed and shaved if and when he needed to. Being a sheep farmer, his clothes were covered in oil from the sheep's wool and he answered to the name of Rabb.

When we were driving up a single narrow track, we had to pull over to let a Land Rover pass and as both cars met, my driver and I both said, "That's him, that's Rabb." We were unable to give chase, as there was no room to manoeuvre the car, so we decided to continue about our other business around the Glen and pursue our visit to Rabb later.

Having had a successful two hours in the Glen, we decided to visit Rabb's sheep farm, so up the hill we ventured. There were large stones and puddles of melted snow to be avoided carefully, as the track was very bendy, and the higher we got, the worse it became.

On reaching the farm, it was as rough as it comes. There were tumbled down sheds, due to neglect and lack of maintenance; the farmhouse was the same and had no electricity or any modern amenities. In fact, the place was so bad with mud, etc., we decided to turn around, go back down the hill, and forget the whole thing.

We stopped at a small shop in Crathie and lo and behold, who drives up with his Land Rover? Sheep farmer Rabb. So, an introduction was made and conversation was started in the old Doric language. He was over the moon and relaxed, he was chatting away as if we had been friends for a lot of years.

Rabb explained that his mother was the last woman in the Glen to speak Gaelic and we also talked at some length about his life on the sheep farm on the opposite side of the Glen from Crathie Naird. He confirmed to us that the house where John Brown was born was the long house that is still standing today at Crathie Naird Farm. The house was thatched and in Rabb's seventy-three years in the Glen, he can remember when the corrugated iron roof went on. He also recalls that these long houses were built with thick stone walls and half of the house was shared with the livestock.

Rabb also confirmed that when John Brown was five years old, the Brown family moved a short distance up the Glen to an 18-acre croft called Brae Neach; the location can still be seen today although it's just a rubble of stones in a field just north of Bridgend of Busil. The last person to live there was a shepherd who fed his dogs, locked them up for the night, then set out for Crathie; the shepherd mysteriously disappeared and so did his life savings. Rabb recalled that, at the time, it was supposed to be a murder investigation, but nothing was ever found.

Rabb used a saying when he parted and it is one that we have heard time and time again, "Good luck with your research. You understand, there are things I can help you with and things I can't." What did he mean and what was he trying to say? Was he telling a story or telling us to look elsewhere? Why still is there truth, but only as much as leads you to another area without revealing too much?

Rabb's mother was Jean McDonald. She was brought up at Mar Lodge where her parents were gamekeepers.

The Thoughts of a Direct Descendent
Great, Great-Grandchild of the Prince

All information held within this book is based on factual information and the information passed on by family members through the generations. At no point in time are the contents herewith written with the intent to offend or embarrass any party or parties involved directly or indirectly. There is no deviation from what is known in order to give benefit of interest to the reader and create a more palatable document compilation. The contents are merely what have been whispered for years within our family in fear of retribution if openly revealed.

Due to the modern day attitudes of most for freedom and well being of family, friends, and countrymen, it is hoped that this information is taken in good spirit and reflects the suppressive nature and lack of understanding the couple would have been subjected to in those times, which led them to conceal so much during their lives.

A private life with loved ones around is not a shameful thing, but a chance to grasp life in both hands and enjoy the pleasures provided, which is understood better in modern days. There is also a better understanding of having children out of wedlock and the required responsibilities of parenthood. It is, however, disappointing that there was no recognition at the time for the hidden prince regarding his father's wealth and royal purse revoked with the death of his parents. The legacy of the "Prince John" was unattainable by spoken word, position in society, or wealth, but remained within a real brave heart that was able to go through life as a common working man in every day reflections of knowing his true birthright and bloodline.

Due to the heavy burdens on royal lives, it was indeed a blessing to give John Hanton freedom from that reign and royal responsibilities to live a normal life, but the knowledge of such has haunted all the knowing family members to this day, silently wishing to tell the story, but wishing for nothing in the way of recognition.

There has been so much written, documentaries made, and the movie, *Mrs. Brown*, in which Billy Connelly played the part so well, but this did nothing more than feed fuel to the fire with a need for the truth to be known.

Auctions on artefacts, sale of properties, with numerous accounts of people trying to make tall of the whispers, looking to cash in on such matters, and, in most cases, they have succeeded, even in bribery, it is claimed.

Although there are details here about the royal couple that would have shocked the nation in those times, it would be preferred to look at them as heroic in their abilities to suppress their love in the prying eyes of politicians and press of the day and still maintain a private life of sustained happiness.

The respect for our Royal Family from then and now should never falter within our people and although there are higher expectations put on them due to their stature and standing, they are always ridiculed at every corner by gossip mongers and paparazzi. This is expected to a point, but it is hoped they all have peace and a breath of normality when they come up to their highland home in Balmoral, even to this day.

To meet with them and pay my respects would be a great privilege, but unfortunately not something I could foresee.

Best regards from,
Another loyal Scottish servant

Norman MacLeod's Bust

"We leave you with a gift to view,
Before you judge what's right and true,
There may be more that time will tell,
By grace of God and all being well,
We may conclude our story's trail,
But be assured, 'It's nae cald kale.'"

Closed Doors and Questions

1. Why is the Hanton family still remaining silent? Is it really an oath they took or are they scared of something?
2. Why did the McCombies of Tillie Fowrie have Alford's cattle named similar and the same as some of Victoria's horses? Was he in on the secret? Was it a private joke or were they a "laughing stock"?
3. Why is there no record of John Brown being in the Queen's service at Balmoral? (We received a letter stating this from parties acting on behalf of the Royals.)
4. Why is there no record of Margaret and Mary Leys being employed as housemaids at Balmoral? (We received a letter stating this from parties acting on behalf of the Royals.)
5. Who gave Margaret Leys the money and who advised her to bank and invest in a foreign bank?
6. What inspired the children's book written by Norman McLeod called the *Gold Threads*, which is about a little lost prince in the woods?
7. Why, in this day and age, were my companion and I sworn to secrecy as to who showed us the marriage bans and where they are kept?
8. Why, to this day, the marriage location must remain a secret and, once again, my companion and I sworn to secrecy?
9. What damage could it possibly do if any of the secrets were to be made public?
10. We asked for a copy of Queen Victoria's will, were told it is not available to the public, and all doors were closed to us.
11. Why are various people in Crathie and Ballater still scared to mention the marriage and Prince John, but some know the secret and won't talk about it, but will always point us in another useful direction?
12. Why would Queen Victoria be buried with a lock of Brown's hair, a picture of him, and his mother's ring given to Victoria by Brown?

13. The published diary of the Liberal MP, the first Viscount Harcourt, for February 17, 1885, related a secondhand story told to his father, the then Home Secretary, by a renowned gossip, that on his deathbed in 1872, the Reverend Dr. Norman MacLeod, the chaplain to Queen Victoria stated that he had conducted a marriage ceremony between John Brown and Queen Victoria.
14. Why did a Royal Minister state that this story may come out at some point, but it was too big for us to safely handle? What was meant by that? The *Daily Mail* on September 2, 2006, reported a similarly second-hand story in which a late senior member of the Royal Family had said that documents confirming a marriage had many years earlier turned up in the Royal archives at Windsor, and is said to have been destroyed.
15. Why would Brown be able to openly correct the royal children as a servant? (Prince Edward got a wooden spoon over the back of the head.) Maybe as he was the man of the house? Even in Edward's adulthood, they openly quarreled, which seems strange of Brown to not fear for position or other consequences. There is only one reason why he would get away with such behavior.
16. Victoria's children to Albert openly referred to Brown as "Mama's Lover," so were they kept from the reality and complete truth also?
17. Why was Brown such a threat to Edward that he had to get rid of all that he set eyes on and was subject to such scandal as the letters retrieved by "blackmail" seemingly from George Profiet by his messenger Sir James Reid? Maybe because it was highly probable the letters would expose the truth?
18. Why were Michael MacDonald and publishers warned off from publication of his papers and findings? Hitting a Royal nerve may be the answer of the day.
19. Why would Edward Stanley, 15th Earl of Derby, write in his diary that Brown and Victoria slept in adjoining rooms "contrary to etiquette and even decency."

Obviously, not privy to the truth of the matter, we may only presume.

20. Victoria shortly after Brown's death, reveals to Viscount Cranbrook the true extent of the loss:

    "Perhaps, never in history was there so strong and true an attachment, so warm and loving a friendship between the sovereign and servant ..... Strength of character as well as power of frame, the most fearless uprightness, kindness, sense of justice, honesty, independence, and unselfishness combined with a tender, warm heart ... made him one of the most remarkable men. The Queen feels that life for the second time has become most trying and sad to bear deprived of all she so needs ... the blow has fallen too heavily not to be very heavily felt..." Why would she pen such deep wording other than feeling the need to communicate her love for her husband and release some pain?

21. What information was leaked enough so as to give the press of various countries the very swift sniff of such a marriage and secret child? A good example would be the cartoons from the satirical magazine *PUNCH*.

22. Whatever happened to John Brown's Diaries? They must be somewhere.

23. Would there be a big missing part to Queen Victoria's diaries for 1861?
    Also, areas of less than seamless diaries in other significant areas? It proves so far to be very much like it?

24. After John Brown died in 1883, it was recorded in Lytton Strachey's 1921 biography of Victoria that a gold broach pin was designed by the Sovereign herself with the initials J.B. flanked on one side of his profile and the Royal Monogram on the other. This is said to have been given to all the Highland servants and personnel on their estate to be worn along with a scarf on the anniversary of his death. Speaks for itself, don't you think?

25. How many Royal decrees are there from Victoria relating to John Brown that still remain in place to this day?

26. Did John Brown really die intestate, or is there a will that has been removed from prying eyes? Hard to believe a man of such standing made no will and testament.
27. Is there not a man amongst us that will come forward and speak the truth? So much circumstantial evidence can be brought forward in support of what has been written here, but we stop at number twenty seven to mark the day in March when John Brown passed away—leaving all you budding enthusiasts to search on another day. But, due respect for the "Hidden Prince" and company, it takes a bigger man to walk away and let it lay than to fight another day.

For a' that, an' a' that,

Bill Rennie

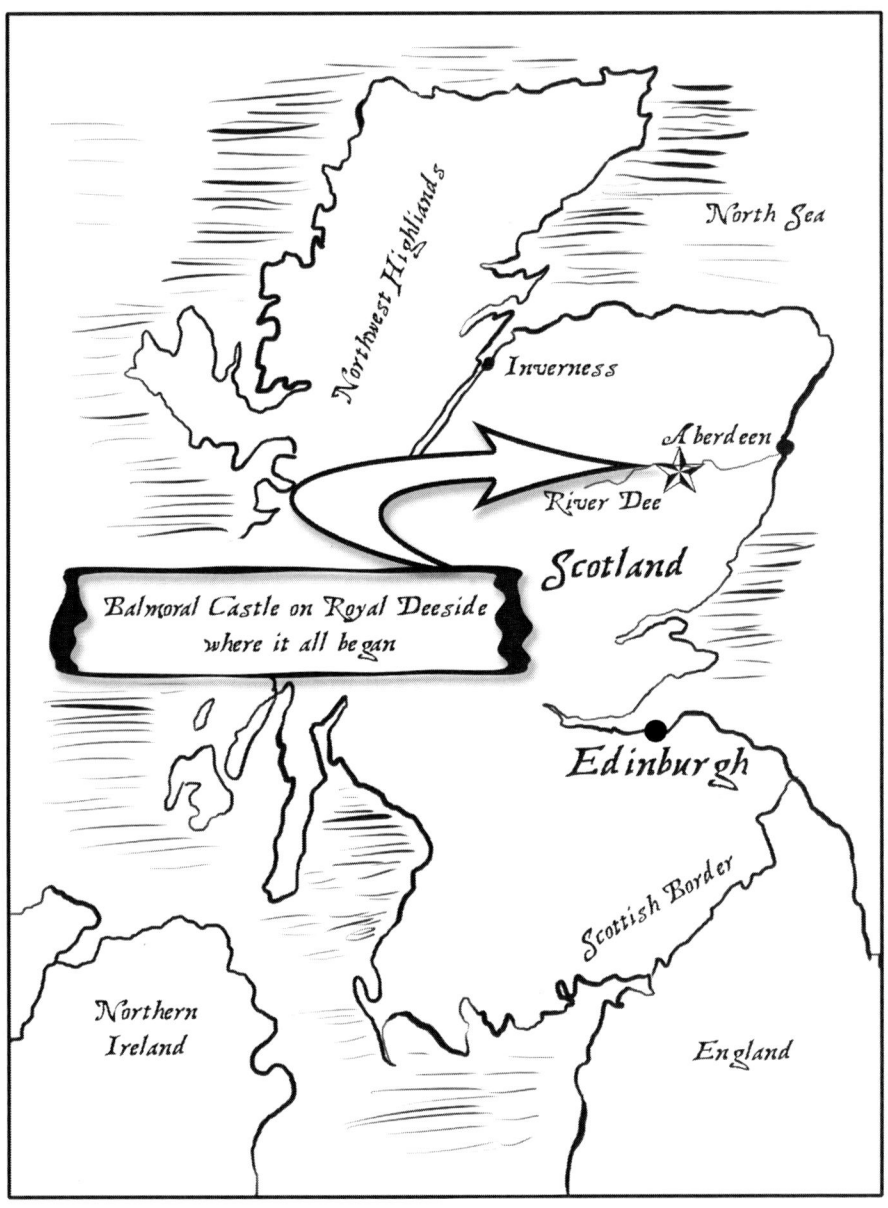